THE
MOMMY
MAFIA

*The Urban Dictionary
of Mothers*

L. J. CHARLESTON

New York

THE MOMMY MAFIA
The Urban Dictionary of Mothers

Published in New York, New York, by Morgan James Publishing. Morgan James and The Entrepreneurial Publisher are trademarks of Morgan James, LLC. www.MorganJamesPublishing.com

The Morgan James Speakers Group can bring authors to your live event. For more information or to book an event visit The Morgan James Speakers Group at www.TheMorganJamesSpeakersGroup.com.

FREE eBook edition for your
existing eReader with purchase

PRINT NAME ABOVE

For more information,
instructions, restrictions, and
to register your copy, go to
www.bitlit.ca/readers/register
or use your QR Reader to scan
the barcode:

ISBN 978-1-61448-548-3 paperback
ISBN 978-1-61448-549-0 eBook
ISBN 978-1-61448-860-6 audio
ISBN 978-1-61448-859-0 hardcover
Library of Congress Control Number:
2013945576

Cover Design by:
Chris Treccani
www.3dogdesign.net

Interior Design by:
Bonnie Bushman
bonnie@caboodlegraphics.com

In an effort to support local communities, raise awareness and funds, Morgan James Publishing donates a percentage of all book sales for the life of each book to Habitat for Humanity Peninsula and Greater Williamsburg.

Get involved today, visit
www.MorganJamesBuilds.com.

Habitat
for Humanity®
Peninsula and
Greater Williamsburg
Building Partner

CONTENTS

MEET THE MOMMY MAFIA

L J Charleston

The politics of motherhood are complicated; yet also highly amusing. Pre-motherhood, it is difficult to imagine a world where a woman's worth is frequently measured by her child's milestones.

"Tom isn't walking yet? Ha-ha! My Andy was walking at nine months!" It's a secret woman's business that is so secret, few women would dare tell a man what *really* goes on.

My first inkling the Mommy Mafia existed was when I found myself in a crowded doctors' waiting room with two-week old twins asleep at my feet. The room was filled with mothers talking a mile a minute, looking proud, frazzled, drowsy, worried, lonely, bored, happy, and totally kaput. It sounded like a nightclub without the music, without the sexual tension, without the fun, yet still, quite entertaining. Within moments of my arrival a woman holding a toddler screeched at me.

"You must *never* carry the babies in those removable car seats. Don't you know that the angle they lie in means they're at risk of having their respiratory tracts cut off?" she said.

Before I had a chance to reply, she found something else that I was doing 'wrong'; my babies were dressed in matching white jumpsuits. She told me I should *never* dress twins in the same clothes because they will have identity problems. "You're encouraging other people to treat them as one person," she said. *I'd just met Dictator Mom.*

A woman sitting beside me was looking terrified. When I asked her if she was okay and she grabbed her little darling and said, "My boy is very sick. He's had a runny nose for five days. I'm sure he has something incurable. This is my third trip to the doctor this week. Maybe I should take him to casualty?" she said.

"I'm sure he's fine. I mean, he looks okay to me. Not that I'm a doctor," I said, speaking softly. But she ignored me, running out the door, presumably straight to casualty. I imagined, with every step she took, she was already planning his funeral. *Exit ER Mom.*

Behind me a woman was holding a potty seat in one hand, a little girl in the other. What was going on? Before I had a chance to ask her, she read my mind. "There is no way I will let her sit on anybody else's toilet seat. She might catch something." *Hello, Germ Phobic Mom.*

I slid back in my chair, extremely thankful that both twins were fast asleep. I'd only caught a couple of hours shut-eye the night before as the moment I got one baby to sleep, the other baby would wake up crying. There's nothing amusing about having to deal with two screaming babies at 2am. I couldn't imagine how easy it must be to get up in the night and breastfeed just one baby! Still the clichés are true; twins mean double love. As I was smiling at my babies, a woman asked, "Did you give birth *naturally*?"

"No, I had a caesarean." That was all the ammunition she needed. "*Why* did you have a caesarean?" she asked.

"Well, if I didn't, one of the twins would have died. He was a footling breech," I said, almost apologizing. But then she launched into a lecture about sky-rocketing caesarean rates. "All these women are too posh to push. I think that's disgusting" she said, slapping her thigh for emphasis. *Meet the Natural Birth Interrogator Mom.*

Imagine if Motherhood is akin to the Mafia, which 'family' would you belong to? Are you Organic Mom ("Don't you realize cow's milk contains chemicals that will kill your child?"), Horny Mom ("Isn't motherhood a good time to start sleeping around?") or ER Mom (if her child sneezes, he is sent to hospital). Perhaps you are Wikipedia Mom (she thinks she knows everything), Chardonnay Mom (she'll always pop open a bottle so long as it's after midday) or Abduction Mom (her kid is attached to a leash - he might get kidnapped, you know).

I confess to belonging in several categories: I personally am Olympic Mom (it's hard not to feel Olympian when you pop out two babies at once), I also have traces of Over-Achiever, Outdoors and the dreaded ER Mom. .. my kids have seen the hospital emergency room several times in their young lives (ahem, a 'spider bite' that ended up being a scratch).

The Mommy Mafia is a comical and insightful look at the fascinating sub-culture of mothers that not only gives people a chance to poke fun at the mothers in their lives…but gives mothers a chance to laugh at themselves.

www.themommymafiabook.com

www.themommymafiabook.blogspot.com

The Mommy Mafia is everywhere. They show no mercy. Just when you think you're doing a good job (kids are happy, food is nutritious, house is spotless, bodies are bathed, faces are kissed) somebody lets you know that something is amiss. Their way is the best way. Your way is not. Beware of the Mommy Mafia. You never see them coming.

It's 8:45 on an ordinary weekday morning, midterm in spring. One by one the Mommy Mafia ventures into suburbia, carrying the weight of their parental responsibilities on their shoulders – apart from Nanny Mom who has sent Helga. The first mom you will notice is Office Mom. What's her DGA or Dead Give Away? She is first in queue at the day-care centre.

"See you kids! Mom's got a 9:15 meeting with the board, followed by a long lunch and another meeting. If I'm home before eight, I'll read you a bedtime story," says Office Mom.

∽

OFFICE MOM

(Dead Give Away – DGA –
she is not wearing sweat suit pants)

∽

Office Mom is always dressed to the nines and in a mad hurry. She is highly organized; the only chit chat she'll have with other moms is about how busy they are, or stressed about work, or running late for a meeting with the boss. Time for a quick kiss, a fleeting feeling of guilt as her child is left with carers for the day and off she goes. She likes to tell herself that she has more quality time with her kids than the women who are with their kids all day. Why? Because working moms get home at 6pm, they have a precious 1-2 hours with their little darlings. In that brief time, they give them their undivided attention, cooking together, eating together, reading, homework, cuddles on the couch. Yet, they reason, a stay at home mom who is with her kids all day, will have to juggle all of that with housework and activities ,so her time with her kids isn't as intense. Office Mom loves to justify day-care by saying, "Oh, it's good for them, they love it! Plus it helps them develop socializing skills".

On the rare occasion that Office Mom is in a playground, you can spot her because she will be the only woman *not* wearing sweats/shorts/t-shirt/husband's baggy shirt to cover the mommy tummy – and she is pushing her kid on the swing with one hand, using the other hand to hold her smart phone. Office Mom tells Housewife Mom that they have it easy.

"Being at work is much tougher than being with kids all day," said Office Mom. At home, you are the boss. At work, you have to put up with back-stabbing, politics, office affairs, fending off advances from amorous male workmates (if you're half-attractive) or feeling rejected if trying to lure a male workmate who barely gives you a second glance. Office Mom likes to lecture Housewife Mom that women should be out there expressing themselves, using their talents and getting rewarded for their labors. Of course, Housewife Mom defends herself (if they can be bothered) by pointing out they have already had 20-plus years of using their talents and stimulating their brains *before* their kids arrived and what's a few short years of enjoying kids while they are young (if you're financially able to). The debate over who has it tougher will never end.

"I *always* get the best parking space. So what if I'm blocking in a few other cars?" says Drop Off Mom.

∞

DROP OFF MOM

(DGA – her car keys are dangling around her neck for a quick getaway)

∞

Drop Off Mom will park anywhere she likes; blocking in as many cars as possible, just to ensure her little darling is at ballet/school/daycare on time. She can be seen casually strolling back to her car, gossiping along the way without a care in the world, despite the strong crowd of parents waiting for her to move so they can claim their 45 minutes of child-free time. The most efficient Drop Off Mom will turn up to school half an hour before the kids are supposed to be there, just so she can grab the best car space. One Drop Off Mom admits to getting an adrenaline rush the moment she spots a prime position for her car. These women usually have very selective deafness. She is oblivious to the sound of other cars honking horns, or mothers yelling at her, in a fruitless bid for her to either push off or, at least, park legally. She loves to brag to other moms that the 'parking fairies' are her best friends.

If anybody is brave enough to tell her that she is selfish, she will explain that her actions are not selfish; she is merely doing her best for her children. It's hard to argue with that kind of logic. Her car is covered with dents and scratches – war wounds from the desperate manoeuvrings as she attempts to get her car into tight spaces. Drop Off Mom is one of the most unpopular moms of all. These women usually own enormous SUVs for maximum intimidation. It doesn't matter who she annoys, so long as she gets the perfect spot.

"For God's sake woman move! I'm late for toddler yoga," shouts Extra-Curricular Mom.

❧

EXTRA-CURRICULAR MOM

(DGA – her kids have dark rings under their eyes due to exhaustion from multiple activities)

❧

E xtra-Curricular Mom signs her kids up for everything; from baby gym, to swimming, to ballet, to paint classes. She feels the pressure of having to do everything for her children – often she is an only child, so Extra-Curricular Mom wants to give him/her the best of the best. Flamenco dancing, baby gym, swimming lessons, jitterbugs music classes, toddler fitness, karate; anything to fill up the time. "Sometimes kids just like to be at home!" cries Agoraphobic Mom. The offspring of Extra-Curricular Mom are always so exhausted by the time they get home, they are near comatose, begging for bed. There is no time for spontaneity. Kids have activities straight after breakfast. They are taken from the kitchen table to baby dance classes, library reading time, craft, home for lunch and, if there is time before the next class, perhaps a quick nap.

It's worse as the kids get older because the variety of activities increases; jazz ballet, piano, flute, oil painting, soccer, football. For girls, grooming and etiquette, for boys, sporting codes of conduct. There are also French lessons, cooking class, guitar lessons; some even teach kids the dying language of Latin. Usually Extra-Curricular Mom does not work, yet loves to tell other mothers how 'busy' they are when all they are doing is ferrying kid from one activity to another and complaining about (but secretly loving) being the 'mommy taxi'.

"I'm signing my daughter up for Flamenco dancing too," says Agoraphobic Mom. "But, of course, the teacher has to come to me."

∾

AGORAPHOBIC MOM

(DGA – she doesn't own a car.
Where would she go?)

∾

Agoraphobic Mom lives in a cocoon of motherhood. She will not come to see you; you have to visit her. They are the Mommy Princess, in self-imposed exile from their former world. Their life revolves around the home. Most Agoraphobic Moms have fancy play equipment installed in their back yards so they have no reason to visit the local playground. One Agoraphobic Mom put her three week old baby into her car for an outing to the supermarket. The baby screamed for the duration of the five minute drive and so she vowed *never* to put her in the car again. And two years later, she still hasn't. Agoraphobic Mom is usually very successful in making other Moms feel that *they* must be doing something wrong by subjecting their kids to the dangers of the outside world.

Agoraphobic Mom's idea of a nightmare is a day-trip to the country. Anything longer than ten minutes in a car and this mother is at her wits' end. Plus, if she actually made it all the way to the countryside, she would panic about being so far from the comforts of her house. One of the biggest challenges for these moms is when their little darling starts school. For some, the fear of doing multiple trips in the car to the school yard, the soccer field, the supermarket and then a friend's house, enough to give her a mighty migraine. This woman is addicted to shopping on the internet. She spends up on eBay as it's the only way she can get her shopping fix, because there is no way she would enter a real store. And, of course, she shops for groceries online and gets a rush when the supermarket delivery man staggers up the driveway with her multiple boxes. On the positive side, Agoraphobic Mom will usually try anything once - but once only. She quickly realizes her life is a lot easier if everything, and everyone, comes to her. At least she knows her limits.

"I'm off to the gym, dropping into the office, then whipping up a dinner for six, writing a proposal for a romance novel and then making dress-ups for the school play," says Over-Achiever Mom.

ᦂ

OVER-ACHIEVER MOM

(DGA – when she walks, she leaves skid marks)

ᦂ

These are the ultimate Super moms. They work, they work-out, they write books, make jewelry, organize market days, their kids are perfect, their homes are immaculate…but do they really exist? Over-Achiever Mom usually juggles multiple kids, multiple activities and spends as much time on their own recreational things as their kids. They also do a lot of baking. You'll never see them buying muffins from a bakery because their home made beauties taste better than anything you can buy at a store. She even decorates the muffin wrapper with unicorn stickers and has been known to bake 100 of them for the local church to sell for $2 each as a fund raiser.

The only people to feel sorry for in this house are the kids. Not *now* – but when they hit puberty. Imagine trying to live up to the reputation of such a magnificent mother? But, strictly speaking, these women are a rarity. You might think you know an Over-Achiever Mom but discover she has an eating disorder. *Not perfect.* You might meet another and realize she's an alcoholic who conceals her vodka in her take away coffee cup so nobody can see that she was drinking at 10am in the middle of a playground. *Not perfect.* If you meet a mother that you suspect might be an Over-Achiever Mom, look again. Remember; if you envy somebody it means you don't really know them.

"See you at the gym!" says Buns of Steel Mom. "I'd rather work out than do *anything*! Oh, apart from shopping for diet shakes and multi-vitamins."

BUNS OF STEEL MOM

(DGA – arms like Angelina Jolie in *Tomb Raider*)

Come hell or high water, Buns of Steel Mom lets *nothing* get in the way of her workout, even if it means leaving her kids in the car while she's on the treadmill. Everything revolves around her exercise routine. The toddler's only social activity is in the gym crèche where he is forced to go twice a day, morning and afternoon. At midday he goes home for lunch and a nap. Sure, he doesn't get to go to the park and have fun with his mom, but so long as she has buns of steel, who cares? Her biggest fantasy is when all her kids are at school and she can spend the greater part of the day at the gym; a pump class here, water aerobics there, Pilates and then weights. It's tough being a Buns of Steel Mom. She gets so many compliments about her hot body that it's water like off a duck's back. She is also very snobby about gyms and will grill other moms about what gym they belong to. She also quizzes other women about what exercise they do; if they do any at all. If a mom says, "I don't have time to exercise," the Buns of Steel Mom is proficient at coming up with a list of other things the unfit moms find time to do, such as Coffee Mom (who 'wastes' an hour a day in a cafe) and her friend Chardonnay Mom (who is on first-name terms with local bartenders).

Many Buns of Steel Moms have ulterior reasons for spending so much time at the gym; they are either having affairs or are besotted with their fitness trainers. One Buns of Steel Mom has been sleeping with her fitness trainer since the birth of her third child. He has absolutely no idea she is a mother. One day she was about to get into her car with the kids yelling in the back seat and he comes over and says, "Tracey!! Are these *your* kids?" and she said, "Oh my God, I'm going crazy, I thought this was *my* car, it's the exact same model but guess what? I *walked* today... see you later!" She walked away and hid around the corner until her fitness trainer was inside the gym before reclaiming her car, her kids and her other life.

"I wish I had time to work out. I'm off to the office," says Work from Home Mom. "Only my office doubles as crèche."

WORK FROM HOME MOM

(DGA – she's wearing sweat pants but she has just as many stress wrinkles and grey hairs as Office Mom)

Work from Home Mom believes she has it the *toughest* as she is forced to endure the boiling pot of work and motherhood in the one space! These moms feel they are failing at both; they can't concentrate on their work because the kids are yelling... but the kids are yelling because they're being ignored while mom is trying to work! One Work From Home Mom locked her kids in their playroom while she was on a conference call but the kids banged on the door and yelled, "Let us out!" for the duration of the phone call. Later, her client sent her an email: "I hope you've let the children out of the closet!" There is always pureed food and sticky fingers over her work space. She relies on the 'electronic babysitter' and panics if a DVD finishes before her online conference call. There are only so many times you can put *The Wiggles* on repeat while you finish a report.

Another Work From Home Mom accidentally wrote out the words to the theme song from *Dora the Explorer* that was playing in the background, instead of writing a marketing report. One report was filled with '2k4j5iu49ierk' due to having a toddler play on the keyboard while mom was in the bathroom. Her kids know that when mom is busy working, they can get away with anything. "Mom, can I have a bag of chips?" "You can have *five* bags of chips... just Shut Up and let me work!"

"There's no way I'd be stuck in an office all day. Who wants to go hiking in the national park?" asks Outdoor Mom.

∽

OUTDOOR MOM

(DGA – she struggles to be at home with the kids. Her solution: she is never at home)

∽

Outdoor Mom is always on the go. Her baby has to snatch whatever sleep he/she is able to get in the car in between social outings. Her diary is filled with morning teas, lunches, shopping trips to far away suburbs. She heard about a new clothing store two hours away. Not a problem. Just haul the kid into the car and off we go! Housework is neglected because she is rarely at home. This woman usually has a cleaner who works on the house while she is out and about. One Outdoor Mom regularly takes her kids on 'day trips' which means leaving the home about 7:00am and returning twelve hours later.

This mom believes the kids have to fit in with her life and if they have to come with her to an audition/job interview/cafe, then so be it! Her kids are trained and/or bribed into sitting in boardroom meetings. She thinks it's better to have your kids with you all the time than put them into day care, so she is an expert at juggling work with kids. In fact, she won't accept a job unless she has a guarantee the kids can tag along. She takes the kids to work functions and thinks nothing of strapping the four year old into a stroller where he sleeps at the cocktail party until 2am. Her issue is that she can't cope with having multiple kids in the house, so she just stays out all day. There is no time to potty train, no time to read to kids, no time to cook a chocolate cake standing at the kitchen bench and licking the bowl; there are too many things to do, places to go!

"I love hiking! But I can't go. See, I've got a facial followed by a pedicure, then I'm having lunch with my ex-boyfriend, but Helga will bring Sebastian to the national park. He just loves Helga," says Nanny Mom.

∽

NANNY MOM

(DGA – she is accompanied by a younger, unattractive woman who is carrying the baby bag and pushing the stroller so her employer can walk hands-free)

∽

Nanny Mom leaves all the work to her nanny, yet still complains and then fires them like they're a dime a dozen. When it's 'Special Friends Day' at school, these women send the nanny. They have to ask the nanny what the kids are 'into' these days; from food to games, toys and books. Many of these moms do not work. They need a nanny to help with the housework, take kids to and from school, make their lunches and baby-sit the toddler so mom can go to the gym. It's almost a status symbol. Yet, it isn't. Most Nanny Moms go out of their way to employ a plain, frumpy nanny so the husband doesn't find her appealing. One Nanny Mom claims she put locks on the bathroom door when her husband kept 'accidentally' walking in on the nanny when she was in the shower. If Jude Law could cheat on then-girlfriend Sienna Miller with his kids' nanny then how can a non-movie star mother compete?

The offspring of Nanny Moms are usually very well behaved...for the nanny. But when the mother resumes duties, they tend to play up, leaving the mother to appreciate her nanny all the more. This often results in a pay rise that will last until Helga gets homesick for Berlin; or until she's poached by another unscrupulous Nanny Mom. One Nanny Mom discovered a pair of black lacy underpants in the basket of her toddler's stroller. Apparently the nanny took the toddler with her on visits to her boyfriend's apartment where the child was put in front of a *Doctor Who* DVD whilst Nanny and her lover were busy in the bedroom. Yet this was not the reason she eventually fired her nanny. She fired her because she couldn't stand it when the kids cried, they would run to the nanny for comfort and not their mother. Oh, the betrayal!

"Come on darling, that's not *real* school like what we do at home," says Home School Mom, prising her child's fingers from the school gate as he gazes wistfully into the school grounds.

HOME SCHOOL MOM

(DGA – her kids are school age but they are never at school. Occasionally she hangs out in 'education' section of the book store, or the stationery aisle of the supermarket, stocking up on supplies)

Home School Mom has one rule – school is an unnecessary evil and the only person who is equipped to teach your children properly is YOU! Not only does this mom teach her kids everything from geography to arithmetic, she has a problem letting go of her kids, even if they beg, 'Please mom! Let me go to school. I want to play with other kids!" Home School Mom loves to tell people that she is a teacher, even though she's had no training. There's no need to let her kids interact with other children. Home school kids can happily mingle with other kids at the supermarket and the park. Plus, once a week there is an arranged play date with other home school kids, so they can socialize with their own kind.

Shouldn't they socialize with kids who aren't so secluded from society? No way! They might learn bad language or unnecessary life skills from kids that are shoved into the evil school system. One Home School Mom was horrified when her child went to visit his cousins who attend a regular school. Her son was given a delicious chocolate muffin before being exposed to the word 'jerk'. From then on, Home School Mom decreed future visits must be strictly supervised. But this mother should be admired. Not only must she have the patience of a saint to school her children herself, but she doesn't get a break from her kids – ever!

"I'll join you girls at the park later. I'm just going to drop into the Baby Clinic and weigh Joshua. He's growing so much, he's off the graph! Your kids are so puny they look like newborns next to him!" gloats Olympic Mom.

OLYMPIC MOM

(DGA – she thinks she is wearing a gold medal)

Olympic Mom is the ultimate competitor. If your baby started to talk at 14 months, *her* baby started at 11 months. Everything is a competition; from teething to toilet training. Olympic Moms are not necessarily athletic in a physical sense. But they *are* athletic in every other way. These are the moms that no matter what *your* child has achieved, their child did it earlier, faster, better. If your 12 month old is not walking yet, Olympic Mom will tell you that her child walked at ten months and there must be something wrong with your kid. If your son said his first word at ten months, Olympic Mom's son said *his* first word at eight months. This woman is excruciating.

The only mom that comes close to beating Olympic Mom is Multiple Mom. When Olympic Mom announces that her children were born 12 months apart, a brave twin mother might quip, "Well mine were *two minutes* apart". Olympic Mom might pause for a moment before saying, "Giving birth to two babies is easier than giving birth to one baby because twins are always smaller." Argh!! Olympic Mom also loves talking about her birth stories - these stories always seem to lurch dramatically from one extreme to the other. From, "My labor lasted two days and I had no drugs! I nearly died and had to have a blood transfusion" to, "I just seem to pop these babies out. My body was born to breed! He was born in 45 minutes and two hours later I was back in my pre-pregnancy clothes again". Sleep is another issue that Olympic Moms like to brag about from both extremes. It's either, "My girls never sleep. I'm up and down all night like a yo-yo. I survive on three hours sleep a night!" OR "I have a better night's sleep now that I'm a mom than I ever did when I was without kids. My little angels sleep all night through". Do not try to compete with an Olympic Mom. It's a race you will never win.

"Ah, you've just had a baby? How was the birth? Wait – let me tell you about *mine*, I'm sure my experience was much more dramatic," says All About Me Mom.

∽

ALL ABOUT ME MOM

(DGA – her favorite topic of conversation is herself)

∽

All About Me Mom insists on telling her stories, whether or not you want to hear it. If your kid just spent the day in ER after swallowing half a bottle of nail polish remover, *her* kid was in intensive care for a month after a brain haemorrhage. She is not interested in your story. She wants to tell *her* story. All About Me Mom and Olympic Mom are friends and rivals. Here is a typical conversation between the two ladies.

"OMG, I slept for just *four* minutes last night. Four minutes! Nobody has a baby that sleeps as badly as my kid," says Olympic Mom.

"That's nothing!" says All About Me Mom. "When Nicky was a baby he'd sleep for only ten minutes, then he'd wake up, then it'd take me about an hour to put him down again and he'd sleep for about twenty minutes and then he'd wake up again. Susie was a great sleeper, a dream baby. She slept through the night at five weeks and I'd have to wake her up for a feed. Then when I had Ryan..." continues All About Me Mom. She is one of the only moms with the ability to actually stop Olympic Mom dead in her tracks; not because she can 'beat' her but because she does not *listen* to Olympic Mom – a lesson other moms should learn.

"Let me give you some breastfeeding tips. Okay, I didn't breastfeed my kids... but what I don't know about breastfeeding isn't worth knowing," says Wikipedia Mom.

WIKIPEDIA MOM

(DGA – she knows everything.
Or she thinks she does)

Wikipedia Mom is a walking encyclopaedia on everything to do with fertility, pregnancy, childbirth, raising kids and beyond. You name it; they will tell you all about it - *ad nauseam*. You don't need a baby book. You just need to befriend a Wikipedia Mom. Twins, triplets? Well, she hasn't had them *herself*, but she knows everything about feeding multiples, raising multiples and whether it's psychologically cruel to put twins in separate classes at school. Need tips about recovering from a caesarean? Wikipedia Mom gave birth naturally but she will give you a blow by blow description of what it felt like to be awake for major abdominal surgery. Breastfeeding tips? Wikipedia Mom has an answer for everybody; ask her about mastitis, breast pumps, inverted nipples and whether, in the world of breast milk, size matters.

Even if Wikipedia Mom did not have a natural birth ... never fear. She can still give you a graphic account of how the contractions felt and ways to combat the ever-increasing pain. "You need to chew ice cubes in between contractions. That worked for a friend of a friend. Oh, and don't bother putting Vitamin E oil on your belly. Stretch marks are hormonal. It's a bit like death; if your number's up, you are going down." In fact, she can even advise mothers of autistic children about how to choose the correct learning program for their child and she can describe in garish detail the psychological impact of withholding sex from your husband in the weeks and months following the birth. "Don't let six months go by without 'doing the deed'. Get back on the horse. If you don't, you risk alienating your husband, killing his self esteem and pushing him into the arms of a child-free woman" said Wikipedia Mom.

If your child only sleeps during the day, Wikipedia Mom will tell you how to make him sleep all night long. If your child refuses to eat green vegetables, Wikipedia Mom will have a kitchen drawer filled with recipes aimed at tempting the most stubborn toddler. But make sure you only befriend one Wikipedia Mom. Life is too short for more. It's a little like religion. Why pray at two altars when it's easier to pray at one?

"Did you hear about the woman who accidentally poured hot oil over her toddler's face? Or the little girl whose legs were shredded when her dress got caught in the escalator steps?" asks Horror Story Mom.

HORROR STORY MOM

(DGA – she's always on the verge of telling a macabre story. Plus, she always looks kind of horrified: arched eyebrows, wide eyes and a wide mouth)

Horror Story Mom will tell you the worst case scenario story about every topic related to motherhood; from the birth where a woman's bladder kept popping out with the baby's head, to the killer bug that can attack children with almost zero symptoms. She's been there, done that and wants you to know all about it. She will tell a pregnant woman the story about her cousin's best friend whose baby was stillborn. She will tell a woman with a five month old baby that her neighbor's aunt in Greece had a baby that died of cot death at six months. If your baby is having sleeping problems, Horror

Story Mom will tell you a story about a woman she met on the train who was so sleep deprived from a non-sleeping baby that she ate a dead cockroach, thinking it was a piece of chocolate.

If you're about to take your kids on the ferry to the city, Horror Story Mom will tell you about her grandmother's third cousin who took her baby on the ferry, the kid fell in the water and sank like a brick. "The mother jumped in the water trying to rescue her baby but the water was so filthy, she couldn't see a thing. And then she got sick from swallowing all the oil and muck in the water and developed an eye disease," said Horror Story Mom. You can try telling Horror Story Mom your own horror story but she will always out-gross and out-shock you. She's even more entertaining if she's hanging out with Chardonnay Mom.

"My baby won't sleep. What should I do? Should I try a warm bottle at night? And what's this weird purple lump on his neck? Do you think it's a spider bite? Also he's not crawling yet – what should I do? " asks Clueless Mom.

ᏚᏃ

CLUELESS MOM

(DGA – she's always clutching
a copy of the latest parenting guide)

ᏚᏃ

C lueless Mom is always asking other moms for advice; suffering from a constant feeling of incompetence and needing reassurance. If they have even the slightest trouble with breastfeeding you will find Clueless Mom on the Breastfeeding 24 Hour Hotline. She loves to drop into the Baby Clinic for advice; "Why is my baby's poo green?" and "What's that funny gap on top of his head?" Clueless Mom has not worked since having kids 12 years ago and claims to have 'no time' to glance at a newspaper or magazine. If there is a cyclone alert, or a major celebrity death, Clueless Mom hasn't got a clue. But, mostly, she is clueless about motherhood.

Clueless Mom likes to confront moms in shopping centres about things such as a strange rash on her baby. "What is this rash? Do you think I've been eating too much chocolate? It must have gone through my breast milk and given him a sugar allergy?" Stranger Mom says, "I'm not a doctor. But it looks like heat rash. You've got him in a jumper on a stinking hot day!" This exchange leads to a new paranoia about over or under-dressing her baby. Most Clueless Moms are married to control freak husbands who give her 'pocket money' each week because they don't trust her to manage her finances. These women can barely think for themselves, let alone think for their kids.

If her kids are not doing enough homework, she gets stressed that they are falling behind the rest of the class. If her kids do too much homework, she is worried that they are missing out on their childhood. "My poor girls are stuck inside all afternoon working on a speech about the national flag. Surely they should be climbing trees and kicking a football instead? Or should I get them to do a bit of homework and then a bit of playtime. Somebody tell me what to do!" moans Clueless Mom. She also worries about whether her kids are getting too much sun, so she has them wear enormous hats and slaps two layers of sunscreen over their arms, legs and faces...then she worries that they are not getting enough Vitamin D.

"Just give him breast milk and he'll be fine. Breast is best," says Breastfeeding Supremacist Mom.

BREASTFEEDING SUPREMACIST MOM

(DGA – her five year old lifts up
her blouse and says "I want booby")

Breastfeeding Supremacist Mom is still nursing a four year-old and loves to tell other moms how disgraceful they are for breastfeeding for too short a time, or, God forbid, not at all. Her favorite question is, "How long did you breastfeed for?" She delights in the reaction she gets when she admits she's still breastfeeding a giant child. Or, better still, she keeps her mouth shut so she can savour the horrified expression on the faces of other moms when she exposes her breasts so her 'baby' can latch on for a few sips before running off to play Nintendo.

Breastfeeding Supremacist Mom also loves to lecture people about the 'evils' of formula and cow's milk. These women know their stuff. They have done 'extensive research' via Google. Yes, according to them, they are well-read. They can tell you that an infant's digestive tract is designed to metabolize lactose and that human breast milk has twice the amount of lactose of cow's milk. "Bottle fed babies have lower levels of desirable Bifid bacteria, higher levels of pathogenic micro-organisms and have a higher alkaline ph. And formula also causes their poo to smell really, really bad," said Breastfeeding Supremacist Mom.

She is usually a big presence in the Breastfeeding Association and encourages mothers to keep feeding even if they have mastitis and the baby is drinking blood from cracked and bleeding nipples. Breastfeeding Supremacist Mom also likes to make moms who have to stop breastfeeding to return to work early for financial reasons, feel like a failure. One day she was at the park with her friend who had a newborn baby. The friend went to the bathroom and, when she returned, she was horrified to see Breastfeeding Supremacist Mom was breastfeeding *her* baby. "Oh, I hope you don't mind. She was crying with hunger and I didn't know how long you'd be gone." Above all, Breastfeeding Supremacist Moms love to tell one another that the great thing about non-stop breast feeding is that their period has never returned.

"I just hate those moms who are too posh to push," says Natural Birth Interrogator Mom. "You can tell just by *looking* at a child if he had a natural, stress-free birth."

NATURAL BIRTH INTERROGATOR MOM

(DGA – she will ask you how long your labor lasted and, depending on your reply, she will either smile or go for the jugular)

Natural Birth Interrogator Mom is a relatively new breed of mom that gave birth naturally and delights in criticizing mothers who didn't; even when a caesarean is performed in a life-saving situation. She tells pregnant women, "I hope you don't have to have a C-section. It will take away the empowerment of womanhood". One new mother sent an SMS to her Natural Birth Interrogator Mom friend to let her know her baby had arrived and the friend responded with, 'Natural or C-section?' Some Natural Birth Interrogator moms see C-section moms as taking the easy road.

"It's not easy!" says C-Section Mom. "It's major abdominal surgery! The surgeon slices through nine layers of stomach muscle – that's nine layers of stitches. I couldn't sit up without pain for weeks!" "So what!" says Natural Birth Interrogator Mom. "It's still easier than pushing a watermelon through a hole the size of an orange."

The only moms who escape the wrath of Natural Birth Interrogator Moms are Multiple Moms who can always use the excuse, "I had two/three/four in there!" or "One was breech, the other was footling breech. They would have died if I didn't have a C-section!" However some Natural Birth Interrogator Moms will then enquire as to why the doctor didn't just 'turn' those babies? Similar to Breastfeeding Supremacist Moms, Natural Birth Interrogator Moms are usually very well read (via Google). They are so proficient at grilling their C-section sisters that they have a scientific comeback for every excuse C-Section Moms can come up with. Sometimes it is easier to just say, "Yes you are right. I was a scaredy-cat. I just wanted it over as quickly as possible." Only then will this terrifying mother leave you alone.

"Nobody gets to wear a medal around their neck saying, "I gave birth through my vagina," says C-Section Mom.

C-SECTION MOM

(DGA – war wounds)

C-Section Mom loves to tell women who had a natural birth, 'At least my lower region is still in good working order'. They usually have a barrage of comebacks on-hand after countless encounters with their arch rival, Natural Birth Interrogator Mom. "I'm lucky my baby was out quick, safe and sound and I didn't feel nervous about the cord getting wrapped around his neck!" says C-Section Mom, frantically justifying her child's birth. Mostly C-Section Moms feel they have to defend their reasons for having a C-section. "I had no choice! My baby was in distress, I had already had 18 hours of labor and then had an emergency C-section or he would have died. I am *not* too posh to push!" Does anybody really think that having a major operation that one is wide awake for and, shortly afterwards, you are looking after a baby or babies is a walk in the park? Most C-Section Moms are left explaining why they *don't* feel less of a woman, or less empowered than natural birth moms.

The media will tell us that there are women 'out there' who chose to have a C-section because they wanted their child born within a particular star sign. But few women would admit this, so they remain silent, so we are left wondering if this is just another motherhood urban myth. Sadly, even a life/death situation will not be enough of a reason to calm the fury of Natural Birth Interrogator Mom who will find a way to end the conversation with, "Surely your doctor could have done something apart from turning to the knife. If only he wasn't in such a hurry to get back to the golf course."

"You should both stop whining and be grateful you had no trouble getting pregnant in the first place!" cries Fertility Mom.

FERTILITY MOM

(DGA – she lectures young women about the perils of leaving pregnancy 'too late')

Fertility Mom took a long time to get pregnant and tried everything; from acupuncture to fertility drugs to reflexology to IVF. Now she considers herself a fertility expert. She takes an immediate dislike to women who brag, "My husband only has to *look* at me and I fall pregnant". Fertility Mom lets these women know that her road to pregnancy was filled with heartache and their bragging about the easy time they had is akin to a rich man boasting about his wealth to a poor man. Fertility Mom lectured a single friend about the need to start trying for a baby on her 35th birthday. "From your mid-thirties your chances are getting slimmer every day. Don't waste valuable time, start trying... Now!" insists Fertility Mom. Then, when that friend took her advice and got pregnant right away, Fertility Mom stopped talking to her. She is a wealth of information for women who are trying to get pregnant. "Use egg whites as a lubricant...that worked for me!"

Fertility Moms who went through IVF and got twins are usually very defensive about how they got pregnant. Their theory is that when you have twins, you get sick of people asking you, "Are they natural?" (Sometimes out of rudeness, sometimes out of natural curiosity) due to the misconception that everybody that has IVF gets twins when the truth is the opposite. Yet women who had IVF and only got *one* baby are never asked this question. "It feels like what they're really asking me is, 'Did you need help to get pregnant?'" said one Fertility Mom. Some Fertility Moms never get over their pregnancy struggle and will only hang out with mothers who can relate to their experiences, such is the jealousy they feel about women who had kids easily. One Fertility Mom – who went on to have triplets – kept the pregnancy tester that gave her the good news and framed it. The frame was hanging in the bathroom until one of the kids mistook the tester for a lollypop and it was never seen again.

"All children are precious and the way they got here is irrelevant. What matters is how much they are loved," says Adoption Mom.

∽

ADOPTION MOM

(DGA – zero family resemblance with the kids)

∽

A doption Mom laughs if you tell her that her kids look like her. "That's impossible," she says. "They are adopted." Some Adoption Moms get slightly annoyed when people say the kids *don't* look like her. "You don't have to be biologically related to somebody to love them," she snaps. "Calm down! I was referring to facial features; not love," said Poor Me Mom.

Adoption Mom is on a mission to educate people about the millions of orphans in the world that need a home and that you should be adding to your family – not biologically but via adoption. Few would disagree with them! Adoption Mom has written countless letters to newspaper/magazine editors who make the mistake of referring to Nicole Kidman's/Angelina Jolie's children as their 'adopted children'.

"Dear Editor, there is no need to repeatedly point out that Nicole/Angelina's kids are adopted. They are *her* children. Do you understand?" (Although Adoption Mom secretly thinks these movie stars let the team down by adopting children and then giving birth as well). These moms are often the envy of non-adoption moms because they still have their hot pre-kids bodies and like to suck up compliments about their appearance by saying, "Well that's because I didn't have to give birth!"

"You could try a donor. It worked for me!" says Gay Mom.

∽

GAY MOM

(DGA – two Moms under
one roof. No sign of a man)

∽

Gay Mom has a list of almost-rehearsed responses to the barrage of annoying questions they get from curious straight moms; mostly a variation of 'Did you have sex to get pregnant?" One Gay Mom delights in turning up to kids' birthday parties with her female partner and fielding the initial questions such as, "Who is she? Is that your son's aunty?" Then, when Gay Mom tells the other mothers that the woman is actually her lover, the next question is always, and "Who is the father?" Of course, that leads to a tonne of personal questions. The straight moms want to know if Gay Mom had sex to get pregnant, whether she used a turkey baster, whether she knows the male, whether the male is gay too and whether the kid has ever met the father.

Gay Moms make a great effort in educating their kids that families come in all different forms. But they often dread the day their kids go to school, where the subject of same-sex partners rarely comes up in conversation. When they teach their kids to say, "I have two mommies," they brace themselves for the onslaught of questions at the next Parent's Committee meeting. Gay Moms learn the art of patience faster than most mothers but they are absolutely sick to death of straight moms asking them 'How did you get pregnant?"

"I just love being pregnant. I'd even happily be a surrogate," says Can't Stop Breeding Mom. "I've had so many babies, the birth is so easy. I hardly have to push! Those babies just walk out."

CAN'T STOP BREEDING MOM

(DGA – she drives a minibus to accommodate her seven children. And she's pregnant with the eighth)

Can't Stop Breeding Mom is that strange breed of woman that does not believe in contraception and for whom taking a year off in between pregnancies is something of a sabbatical. Seven kids? No problem. They are usually condescending towards moms who, on average, pop out two or three children. "Only three kids? What's wrong? Couldn't you get pregnant again?" asks Can't Stop Breeding Mom. "Well, we only ever wanted three kids. Isn't that enough?" shrugs Poor Me Mom. "No. Three is *not* enough. You are not doing your bit to help populate the country. I'm not stopping until I have at least five more. Three kids? You're pathetic", says Can't Stop Breeding Mom.

Can't Stop Breeding Moms usually rely on the older children to help raise the younger ones. One Can't Stop Breeding Mom has a roster for her 10, 11 and 12 year old daughters ... the 10 year old prepares the baby bottles, the 11 year old bathes the two and three year olds, and the eldest daughter looks after the rest of them. Can't Stop Breeding Moms usually fall into the extreme categories of being either filthy rich or poverty stricken. One Can't Stop Breeding Mom is pregnant with child number eight and her family is so poor that both sets of grandparents chipped in to buy them a minivan so they can actually leave the house. On the other end of the monetary scale, there is a Can't Stop Breeding Mom who hires a new nanny every time she has a new addition to the family. Their house is so enormous there is a separate wing for the hired help. These moms are harking back to the last century where having eleven kids did not raise an eyebrow. Of course, back then, they had a pretty good excuse – there was no contraception, save for the odd old wives tales that rarely work (such as having sex standing up) which is all they have time for.

"It's irresponsible to have so many kids. You can't give them enough individual attention. Plus, there's the environment to consider and don't get me started about the population explosion," says Dictator Mom.

DICTATOR MOM

(DGA – she's always lecturing some poor soul)

Dictator Mom is always telling other moms what they are doing wrong and what they *should* be doing. Sleep: you need to put aluminium foil on the windows to block out the sun. Baby refusing bottle: you must refuse the breast and let baby go hungry. Then, when he is *really* starving, he will be begging for that bottle. Baby refusing solids: just put him in his highchair surrounded by a variety of finger foods and eventually he will be so hungry or curious, he will eat. She will also lecture Multiple Mom about the importance of separating twins at school. Dictator Mom also likes to lecture moms about speech. "Don't talk for him. Don't use baby language. Use the proper word for train. Don't say 'choo choo'. And don't say 'moo moo', say 'cow'. She also lectures moms about homework. "Never let them do homework on a full stomach. Make them do homework before dinner and tell them they aren't allowed to eat until they are finished their work. You want to be able to hear those tummies rumbling!"

Dictator Mom says you shouldn't buy books for your kids. "Make them go to a library. And you must never, ever let them call an adult by their Christian name. They need to learn to respect authority. If you have sons, make sure they have female teachers so they learn from an early age to respect women." She even likes to tell moms what they should be wearing. "Wear proper clothing for moms – don't ever look frumpy, nor should you look like mutton dressed as lamb. Sweetheart, your days of wearing shorts were over years ago."

"And lose the pacifier," says Pacifier Police Mom.

PACIFIER POLICE MOM

(DGA – she pulls pacifiers from the mouths of babes and throws them in the trash. It's her duty)

Those who have committed the 'sin' of using a pacifier, mostly out of desperation to drastically reduce the volume of a screaming child, would have already met Pacifier Police Mom. These women like to harass mothers whose little darlings use a soother; lecturing them about how bad it is for the shape of their mouths and also giving 'helpful advice' about how to stop your child using a pacifier, including giving the offensive apparatus to the 'pacifier fairies'. "Why does he have a pacifier? He is too *old* to have a pacifier," said Pacifier Police Mom. "He is a bad sleeper," said Poor Me Mom. "Throw it away!" yells Pacifier Police Mom. Here is some other unsought advice freely thrown around by Pacifier Police Mom:

1. Tell your child you are giving the pacifier to Santa, the fairies, the Easter Bunny, even Jesus.

2. You're giving the pacifier to the new babies that really need them.

3. When you're driving, casually wind down the window and toss the pacifier out the window, saying 'Oops, look what mommy has done!" Then you have to convince your toddler that you cannot buy him a new pacifier because the stores have run out.

You will never win a debate with Pacifier Police Mom. She will give you a list of bizarre psychological reasons why a pacifier will have a negative impact on your child's life until death. "Think about what he is sucking on... a plastic nipple! He will always have a nipple fixation and end up being a hopeless sex addict," she says.

Back at the school gates – "Coffee anyone?" asks
Coffee Mom. "My whole morning is clear!"

COFFEE MOM

(DGA – she practically lives at the cafe)

C offee Mom is the woman who, after dropping
an older child off at school, sits in a cafe for at
least an hour, chatting to other moms about
everything from the tooth fairy, sex education and which
stay-at-home Dad is the token 'Hot Dad' in the school
playground. They are very easy to spot. They are the ones
who, as the school bell tolls at 9:00am, turn to each other
and squeal, "Coffee?"

Many of these moms had high-flying, highly stressful
careers and so delight in their new life where they can
take it a bit easier. If you eavesdrop, you will pick up
a bit of legalese from the ex-lawyers or medical know-
how from the ex-doctors. Sometimes there are scandals
amongst the Coffee Moms. One woman had to go back
to full-time work and her husband took a turn being a
house Dad. This Dad was very popular with the ladies

and was the only man allowed in the inner sanctum of the Coffee Mom Club. However, the Dad got a bit too close to one of the moms (Horny Mom) and took their friendship beyond the cafe. They were last seen building a house together with a combined family of seven kids under seven. Naturally, they never went to their favourite cafe again. The majority of Coffee Moms are Older Moms who believe that children – aged from 0 to preschool – actually *enjoy* sitting in a cafe.

"Sarah, you get the afternoon play area ready. Anita, can you do the snacks? Nora, you're in charge of face paints and I'll organize the craft. See you at four on the dot," says Events Manager Mom.

EVENTS MANAGER MOM

(DGA – barking orders, clutching her itinerary. She lives and dies by her itinerary)

Events Manager Mom has brought aspects of her former career into motherhood with spectacular results. She delights in organizing her child's day-to-day activities as though she was chairing a major corporation's AGM. Even the street Christmas party was given a professional touch; Events Manager Mom printed out a rundown of the day's events and a list of neighbors with allocated jobs. What's strange is that Events Manager Mom usually does not irritate other moms, who are very thankful that somebody else has taken over. Hey, it's one less thing for everybody else to think about!

Even a simple trip to the park to meet other moms has to be highly organized. Events Manager Mom will email a rundown of requirements; who's bringing oranges, who's bringing rice crackers and juice, which mother is in charge of ride-on vehicles and who's in charge of the sunshade.

However one Events Manager Mom was horrified when Neat Freak Mom raised her voice and suggested the picnic rug be set up on the grass instead of the dirt. (You know, in case there were germs lurking about.) Events Manager Mom had a hissy fit, throwing away her spreadsheet and telling Neat Freak Mom, "Fine! *You* organize it then!" It was dramatic, it was final. Nobody ever butted in again.

Events Manager Mom is always hanging out with Boot Camp Mom. But it is not a friendship made in heaven. The two women often clash heads over niggling details such as whether lunch should be served at 12:30 or 12:45pm.

"One organic free-trade latte please! Do you have wheat-free carob muffins?" asks Organic Mom.

༉

ORGANIC MOM

(DGA – she wears kaftans and carries a hemp tote)

༉

O rganic Mom lectures everyone about the dangers of non organic food, bed linen and anything with coloring or chemicals. These are the moms who will never give their children anything sweeter than a dried (organic) pear. These children are also the ones who turn up to your house for a play date and gorge themselves on all the 'normal' food in your cupboard. Organic Mom loves to tell other moms about all the bad things the non-organic food you give your child is doing to them. Remember, in her eyes, everything you put on your child's plate is going to give them cancer. Organic Mom doesn't only lecture about food. She also likes to lecture other moms about the bad things they are doing by sleeping their kids in non-organic cotton sheets. And don't you *dare* carry your baby in a sling that is made from non-organic cotton. Don't you realize you are exposing him to harmful chemicals that one day (perhaps when he is in his 80s) might make him ill? Organic Mom likes to turn up to kids' birthday parties and interrogate the host mother about the food she's prepared.

Party Plan Mom was forced to admit that the birthday cake was baked with non-organic flour, barn laid eggs, unnatural food coloring and non-organic sugar. Organic Mom is heard shouting at her daughter, "Skye you are not allowed to eat any of this BAD food". She then produces a lunchbox from her hemp tote and serves her daughter a selection of nuts, fruit and an organic brownie (cooked with carob, not cocoa). This child even gets organic Easter eggs. Organic Moms believe they have the cure for every possible ailment your child might be suffering from. A cold? That's because you haven't 'gone organic'. Headaches, misbehavior, bad skin? You won't get sick if you go organic. Just do it. You'll thank me for it one day. She is like a broken record that will never, ever let up until you tell her (or just lie) that you have forsaken sugar.

"Stop! Does this have nut traces?" asks Allergy Mom.

ALLERGY MOM

(DGA – carries a magnifying glass
so she can easily read the fine print
ingredient list on packaged goods)

Allergy Mom assumes that her darling is allergic to everything known to man from nuts, duck feathers, strawberries, bread, sausages, maybe even hummus. Even though the doctor has told her repeatedly her child is NOT anaphylactic. Anywhere they go where there might be food; Allergy Mom is hovering almost as intently as Helicopter Mom, ready to snatch from her child's mouth any food that looks even mildly suspicious. If there are cupcakes with pink frosting, apparently that is okay. But if the frosting is blue – no way! "The additives in blue coloring are just terrifying. If she takes just one bite – one bite! – she will break out in spots and start to choke!" cries Allergy Mom.

When a mom made a comment about how much she loves being a mother, Allergy Mom interrupted, "It'd be *easy* being a mom if your child is not allergic to *everything*!" If Allergy Mom comes to your house she makes a bee-line to the kitchen where she searches the cupboard for anything that might endanger her darling. It doesn't matter that you have reassured her over and over again there is no peanut butter in the house because nobody in your family actually *likes* it. She will get down on her hands and knees sniffing out that peanut smell. Her child is not actually allergic to nuts but she feels it's better to be safe than sorry. The real anaphylactic moms hate her.

"Thank the nice lady for your babyccino, darling!"
says Politeness Police Mom.

∽

POLITENESS POLICE MOM

(DGA – carries a weathered
copy of an etiquette guide)

∽

oliteness Police Mom delights in teaching other people's kids the fine art of speech. She is not a speech pathologist; she just cannot help correcting the wrongs of newly-talking toddlers. If your child does not say, 'Thank you' when the Politeness Polite Mom gives him an apple/candy/Kleenex, she will take it away from him until he thanks her. "But he is only eight months old. He can't *say* thank-you yet!" says Poor Me Mom. "That's no excuse for bad manners," says Politeness Police Mom. These women expect children – even newborns – to behave in an orderly, appropriate and polite manner. They must not spill their food. They must not yell. They must not stand in front of the television, blocking the view of others, even if nobody else is even watching TV.

Politeness Police Mom takes great delight in keeping all children in line; it doesn't matter if they are the offspring of friends, relatives or perfect strangers. In fact, it's even better for them if they *are* the children of perfect strangers because then they can say whatever it takes to make them behave. Whether your child is tired from lack of sleep, grumpy due to cold/flu or just a whining kid by nature, they will not get away with anything with Politeness Police Mom in earshot. The Politeness Police Moms don't only tell other people's children what to say, they also enjoy telling them *how* to say it. Naturally, the majority of their young victims are children who are just learning how to speak. One Politeness Police Mom corrected a child with a chronic lisp. "If you don't say 'flower' instead of 'thlower' you will *not* get candy." The kid managed to say it properly. Amazingly, she managed to achieve what no speech therapist has been able to do, saving the boy's mother hundreds of dollars. See, the Politeness Police Mom has a purpose after all.

"Oh no! She's got crumbs everywhere. I'll just get the mini vac from the car!" cries Neat Freak Mom.

NEAT FREAK MOM

(DGA – her house is so spotless
you'd never guess children lived there)

Neat Freak Mom actually thrives on spring cleaning. But, for this mom, it's not twice a year, it's twice a day, every day. Many mothers are scared to take their kids to Neat Freak Mom's house. If a child drops even a *crumb* of a cookie, Neat Freak Mom will whip out the vacuum cleaner. She virtually neglects her kids because she is so busy dusting and cleaning up after them. When she does take them out, she brings along a spare set of clothes in case a kid gets even the smallest amount of dirt or food or, God forbid, a blueberry stain on their freshly laundered whites. She doesn't like to take her kids to the park because the park is full of dirt and her kids might get dirty. Her kids would never be allowed to jump in a puddle or roll through the leaves. Her kids are forced to wash their hands with disinfectant at least six times a day; sometimes twice depending on the grime and on whether they have petted a dog, cat or guinea pig.

Her kids are always sick because they're never exposed to 'good germs'. Neat Freak Mom is very particular about which toys are 'outdoors' toys and which are 'indoors' toys. If you take an indoors toy outside, it will bring naughty germs back into the house. This woman is not called Neat *Freak* for nothing – she will totally freak out! Neat Freak Mom cannot handle seeing any food around her toddler's mouth so she's constantly wiping him until the lower part of his face is red raw. She stands close by, a face cloth in her hand; just an inch from her child's chin at all times. In fact, the face cloth is usually in her pocket for any 'emergencies'. She not only has the most expensive designer vacuum cleaner inside the house, she also keeps the mini cordless version for the car where food is banned. But on the rare occasion a child is brave enough to smuggle a muffin in the back seat, she will pull over – even on major highway –to keep her car looking like it did when it left the showroom.

The best thing about Neat Freak Mom is when she comes to your house she can't stop herself from wiping your kitchen bench, picking up toys. She's more than just a friend, she's a free cleaner. You love her.

"Toby, you horrible boy! You've spilled it again,"
yells Mean Mom.

MEAN MOM

(DGA – she doesn't tell her kids off for swearing
because she is always swearing at *them*)

Mean Mom is always shouting at her kids. In fact, they are terrified of her. She will not let them have friends to play after school because she doesn't want extra kids messing up the house. She won't give them afternoon tea or even a glass of water until they have finished their homework and completed a list of chores. She only lets them celebrate their birthday every other year. If she uses a word they have never heard of, such as 'chaos' she will refuse to tell them what it means. "That's what a dictionary is for. I am not a dictionary!" she yells.

Mean Mom would rather a child be told off by his teacher for not bringing a particular book, hat, or project to school if he has forgotten it. Rather than remind him, Mean Mom will wait until the child is at the school gates crying, "Oh no, I've forgotten my hat! Now I won't be allowed to play in the sunshine!" Mean Mom will tell him that it's his own fault; he should have remembered his hat. Would it really kill her to have reminded him before they left home? Yes, it would kill her. She is the Mean Mom.

Her meanness is not confined to children; she also enjoys being mean to other moms. One Mean Mom went to a mother's group morning tea where a first-time mother of twins was struggling to settle two babies at once. Mean Mom told her, "You are a tense, stressed-out mother. Plenty of women have twins and say it's very easy. Also, it is not necessary for you to hold both babies on your lap. You can put one on the floor".

Some Mean Moms also like to practice the art of 'controlled crying' where you let a baby cry for several hours to 'break them in'. One Mean Mom proudly told Fashionista Mom that her three month old sleeps through the night. "That's because, when you do controlled crying, your baby learns that crying won't help because nobody comes. Your baby gave up!" said Fashionista Mom, who was never invited to Mean Mom's house again. Sometimes Mean Mom surprises even herself with the severity of her meanness. She made Playground Groupie Mom cry after lying to her about her whereabouts, sending her on a wild goose chase in a crazy bid to avoid attending the same park at the same time due to a dispute over football that fell into an eel-infested lake.

"Oh, damn. Cheryl's here again. Watch out everyone." "Hi girls!" says Playground Groupie Mom (Cheryl). "What's happening? I've just been chatting to Lyn and Karen at the Park. But they had to leave. They were both late...for something. They didn't say. Oh, is that Lyn and Karen I see over there? I thought they were....Never mind. May I join you?"

PLAYGROUND GROUPIE MOM

(DGA- it's like the parting of the sea
when she appears as everybody runs a mile)

Playground Groupie Mom hangs around the playground striking up conversation with other moms in a desperate attempt to make new friends. Motherhood can be lonely, so it's only natural women congregate around places they can meet other moms. But these ladies take it to the extreme. You might be both pushing your kid on a swing and strike up a conversation about the weather, or potty training. But some moms go one step further and literally stalk the mom they are most 'attracted to' - especially if they have kids of a similar age or both have two boys/two girls. Playground Groupie Mom will ask the woman how often she comes to the playground, what day she comes here and what other parks she visits. Then she will make hints about wanting to join a mothers group or book club in the area. Playground Groupie Mom will take her kids to up to three different parks each day in a bid to meet the 'right kind' of moms.

Most women run and hide when a Playground Groupie Mom approaches them. But these ladies are like mosquitoes that will buzz around you until you are forced to open the doors of conversation and kinship. One notorious Playground Groupie Mom takes great delight in following the mothers she meets at playgrounds to the nearest mall. There she launches into her usual, "Wow, fancy seeing you here! Great minds think alike. I just love these stores. Shall we meet here next week?" Remember, even if you vow to never return to that playground.... when you find a new one, Playground Groupie Mom will find it too.

"Hey, your kid is playing with my kid's tricycle. Give it back! And your daughter's been on the swing for nearly four minutes now. Time's up!" says Playground Police Mom.

PLAYGROUND POLICE MOM

(DGA – She's holding a stop watch)

Playground Police Mom is the unofficial guardian of the swings. She actually times the children (two minutes for a swing); informing their mothers when their 'time is up' so that their own little darling can have a go. Of course, they do not time their own children. Their antics do not stop at allocating swing time. They also stop kids from the unthinkable – climbing up the slippery slide, instead of doing the 'right thing' and sliding down. She lectures children as young as 18 months. "Do it properly!" she yells. She also gets hot under the collar if kids put dirt, pieces of bark, or food at the base of the slide so that kids sliding down get a dirty bottom. She threatened to ban a young boy from the park who tipped his water bottle on the slide.

Most people are scared of Playground Police Mom. She doesn't need a uniform. She is very easy to spot. Playground Police Mom also has rules on general playground behavior. If you momentarily leave your park bench to push your child on the swing, then it's an open invitation for another kid to help himself to it. Ditto with scooters and bicycles. Most people accept that if something is left unattended, it's not a big deal if another child has a play with it. But Playground Police Mom seems to have a sixth sense for knowing which things belong to each child. So if she spies a child riding a scooter that is not his, she will tell him to get off. "You're not allowed to play with toys that don't belong to you!" She will insist on this rule, even if both of the mothers don't have a problem with a child playing with the other child's scooter. Everything bothers Playground Police Mom. If she sees a child holding a stick she will yank it from his hand, even if he was not about to poke anybody's eye out.

Playground Police Moms are usually mothers of girls (mothers of boys are oblivious to boys holding sticks because they are *always* holding a stick). By the time her child is at school, Playground Police Mom morphs into the dreaded School Yard Mom.

"Those little bitches had better play with my Ava today, or I'm going to the Head Mistress and report them all!" says School Yard Mom.

❧

SCHOOL YARD MOM

(DGA – she's the only adult, who is not
a teacher, standing in the playground,
and long after the bell has chimed)

❧

School Yard Mom is so delusional, she thinks she is second wheel to the school principal. She delights in spying on her friend's kids and reporting their misbehavior to the parents. She believes she has the power to hand out detentions and this crazy lady she gives them out like they're candy. Sometimes she tries to be Cool Mom and tells dumb jokes to the kids in a desperate bid for acceptance.

One School Yard Mom overheard a teacher asking kids not to kick a football at the windows in case it breaks. So she yelled at the teacher, "How dare you stop our children from playing ball!" When the teacher told School Yard Mom that she is trying to protect school property and, "Would you like to pay for a broken window?" she stormed off to the principal's office to complain about the teacher. School Yard Mom was probably the outsider in high school and is now trying to make amends for a life less than perfect. Ironically, her actions always backfire because the offspring of Cool Mom will tell their mothers, "Harry's mom was doing yard duty today and told us we had to play with him or we'd get a detention." This usually results in School Yard Mom being called to the office and forced to relive the humiliation of her high school years once again. Advice: School Yard Mom needs to get a life outside of her child's school. Perhaps she can hang out with Coffee Mom at the cafe across the road from the school. This way, the school yard can still be in her line of sight but, hopefully, forever out of reach. At least until the school bell tolls.

"My kids have never climbed a tree, ridden a bicycle or skateboard, they're not allowed in the kitchen or bathroom unsupervised. It's a scary world out there!" says Bubble Wrap Mom.

BUBBLE WRAP MOM

(DGA: her kids have better
protection than the US President)

The Bubble Wrap Mom is worse than the Helicopter Mom. Not only does she hover around her children, she would wrap them in cotton wool, if only she could. They are not allowed to cross the road without her ; not even when the lollypop man is standing guard as the quintessential road warrior. The kids cannot walk just two houses down the street to retrieve a missing football for fear of them falling, being abducted or swooped by a kamikaze blackbird. No! They cannot watch any television beyond 6:30pm for fear of advertisements targeting adults. What if a tampon ad appears and the kids ask 'What the heck is that thing?"

Bubble Wrap Mom was horrified when Thrift Store Mom said her children walk unsupervised for five minutes up the street to buy an ice-cream. Not only was Bubble Wrap Mom shocked about the unassisted stroll in the 'burbs, she lectured her friend about letting them consume a treat that is counterproductive to a regime of healthy eating. Bubble Wrap Mom will only let her kids go on play dates if she is allowed to stay and help the host mom supervise. At the friend's home, Bubble Wrap Mom will stop them from climbing a tree (they might fall) jumping on the trampoline (they might break a leg) or even help cook popcorn (the hot oil might splatter in their faces). She will even prevent them from going to the bathroom, unless it's an emergency, because bathrooms are filled with dangerous utensils like nail scissors. These mothers do not encourage independence and their children become hopelessly clingy.

Most of all, Bubble Wrap Mom likes to stand guard in case another child says something to upset one of her little darlings. The last thing she wants is a psychologically scarred child who might be at risk of being called a 'jerk,' 'dick-face' or whatever name is popular at the time. The offspring of Cotton Wool Moms usually end up being simpering, wimpy adults and we've all had to work with one of those excruciating people, haven't we?

"Oh no, the clouds have disappeared! Quick, somebody throw me that hat! Where's the sunscreen. Baxter, get under that tree NOW!" yells Afraid of the Sun Mom.

∾

AFRAID OF THE SUN MOM

(DGA: her kids are white as ghosts)

∾

A fraid of the Sun Mom only visits the park with her kids on overcast or even rainy days. If it's hot outside, and she absolutely cannot keep her kids indoors, she will make them play in the shade – even if that means spending an hour sitting under a small bush. On a cloudy day at a playground, you will notice Afraid of the Sun Mom. She's the mom who, when the sun was barely peeping through the clouds, pounced on her four year old. "Baxter come HERE!" yelled with the same intensity of a woman trying to get her child away from a dirty old man in an overcoat. Baxter reluctantly edged closer to his mom. This boy knew exactly what was coming. Within moments he was lathered with layer upon layer of the highest sun factor protection on the market. She also refuses to take her kids outside on a sunny day between the hours of 10am and 2pm.

"But, there's hardly any sun," said Dictator Mom. "You're making his skin very greasy for no reason. Does he really need that much protection? All the other kids are playing under cover?" Then came the lecture. Afraid of the Sun Mom (whose kids are NEVER outside without a hat...not even in the pouring rain. I mean, you never know when those clouds are going to clear and the evil sun will make a brief yet deadly appearance). Afraid of the Sun Mom lectured Dictator Mom (a rare occurrence) about skin cancer. Ok, we all know it's deadly. But there are benefits in your kids getting SOME sunshine. It's called Vitamin D. Every ten minutes this woman is wiping cream on her kids face. If you try to tell her that the cream is still there, it's just soaked into the skin, she will look at you like you're an idiot. "I want to be able to SEE the cream so I have peace of mind it is still protecting him."

When a little girl accidentally splashed her Baxter with water, Afraid of the Sun Mom ran towards him with a towel, wiped his face, then she reapplied all that sunscreen. "Why don't you buy the water proof stuff? There's a great organic brand," offered Organic Mom. But it was like talking to a brick wall. So, when the clouds disappeared and the sun shone in full, that's when Afraid of the Sun Mom decided to abandon the playground for the safety of the mall. "We're out of here!" she said, dragging her kid to the safety/shade of her SUV. This woman is only ever happy when it's winter.

"You've got two girls? You poor thing. So, are you going to try for a boy?" asks Boy Mom.

BOY MOM

(DGA – dead bugs and
old batteries in her handbag)

Boy Mom loves to say to Girl Mom, "What a shame you couldn't give your husband a son." These women are usually obsessed with sports and love to quote statistics, such as "Jack can run the 100 meters in under XX seconds." A Boy Mom was overheard saying to her child as he sobbed, "Don't cry...you sound like a girl!" The diehard Boy Moms are so pro-male they've forgotten that they are female.

They get angry when the school hosts a disco as a fundraiser, accusing the school of being too pro-female. "What boy in his right mind would want to go to a disco?" they protest. "How would the Girl Moms like it if we organized a wrestling fundraiser?" Boy Mom is good friends with Scream from the Sidelines Mom and cannot resist yelling to the point of laryngitis at every sporting match their sons attend.

They love to point out the advantages in having boys; when they are older they are busy doing 'boy stuff' with their dad, leaving you to do your own thing. They also like to point out to Girl Moms that girls are not a challenge for women because, being female, at least you have an understanding of the female mind. But when you have boys, well, they're just one big mystery! Boy Mom told Girl Mom that she is glad she didn't have a daughter. "It's just so amazing that my female body produced a male. Where's the magic in having a daughter? All you're doing is cloning yourself!"

"Come on Luke! Pull your finger out and kick the damn ball! I want to see you get a goal! Kick the damn ball! WTF? Hey, Ref! Penalty shootout? That kid needs a red card!" shouts Scream From The Sidelines Mom.

SCREAM FROM THE SIDELINES MOM

(DGA – She can name the player, number and position of every footballer in every code)

Scream From The Sidelines Mom is more than an enthusiastic sports parent. She is obsessed with the idea her child is the next David Beckham. She screams at her child for every goal, every missed goal, every kick and every missed kick. "Liam! You're looking the wrong way! The ball is behind you, you idiot!" Yet, at the same time, she likes the idea of her child being wrapped in cotton wool and gets mildly hysterical if another child's boot ever so slightly grazes his precious shin. This is when Scream From The Sidelines Mom turns her attention to other parents. "Your child is a violent menace to society!"

A Scream From The Sidelines Mom was so angry when her child's soccer team was forced to play against kids two years older that she phoned the club manager to complain and not only did she get an apology and an explanation, she campaigned to get the club rules changed so no other kid would go through the indignity of being beaten by older (more experienced) children. If she dies tomorrow, this will be one of her proudest achievements. Ever.

Scream From The Sidelines Mom is not always a Boy Mom but she is very friendly with mothers of boys and is, in a strange way, living a sporting life through her kids – not that she was ever in a position to play rugby but, perhaps if she had been born male, that would have been her dream. When her son begged her, "Mom, please can I quit football? I'd rather play baseball this year?' Scream From The Sidelines Mom burst into tears, "Mommy will be sooo disappointed if you leave football. Don't do this to me! I hate basketball!"

"I wish I could clone myself. At least I'd have someone to do some of the work. My husband is useless," says Man Hater Mom.

MAN HATER MOM

(DGA – She refers to her
husband as 'the kids' father)

Man Hater Mom blames men for everything. They spend a lot of time bitching and moaning about their male partners; mostly because they either don't help, they help too much, they work too late or get home too early and are 'in the way'. One Man Hater Mom deliberately locked her husband out of the house when he returned from a work function at midnight. She ignored his knocking at the door and he ended up sleeping in the car. She said she wanted to punish him for having fun while she was knee deep in diapers, homework and preparing dinner for four little people.

Man Hater Mom complains about everything male related. It's not uncommon to resent your male partner for leaving the toilet seat up, or for not changing the toilet roll... but these women resent their man for slightly illogical reasons. "I can't stand my husband," said Man Hater Mom. "He leaves his dirty socks and jocks on the floor, he can't even boil an egg and I've decided I'm moving to the guest room." "Why? Does he wear ugly pajamas? Or does he snore?" asked Fashionista Mom. "No. He smells really bad. He just smells very...male," said Man Hater Mom. These women are often confused with Feet up Past 6:00pm Mom who likes to pass everything over to her husband the moment he walks in the door after his 'break' in the office.

"Lucy loves housework. She even has her own broom and a cute little gingham apron," says Girl Mom.

∽

GIRL MOM

(DGA – loose glitter and fairy wings in her car)

∽

Girl Mom enjoys asking Boy Mom, 'Are you going to try for a girl?' holding the strange misconception that every woman must want a daughter to go shopping with. Girl Mom always comments on what other little girls are wearing, "'Wow what a pretty dress! Where did you get it?" she will ask the other Girl Mom. She is over-protective of her daughters to the extent that if a boy comes within an inch of her, she is frightened her girl will be punched, pinched or spat at. A Girl Mom was horrified when her four year old took her clothes off in front of a group of six year old boys. But, instead of yelling at her daughter to put her underwear back on, she yelled at the boys for *looking*.

Girl Mom loves to hang out with Fashionista Mom while they discuss the valuable skills they will pass down to their daughters, such as pancake making and the correct application of lipstick and which current celebrity 'tween' is a good role model for their girls. Some Girl Moms are very competitive about their daughter's dancing abilities. One woman was so angry that her best friend took her daughter out of the Jazz Ballet class they were both attending to join a professional junior's class, that she started a campaign in the media about the dance teacher who had been in prison – she'd served three days behind bars in Egypt when her passport was stolen some 20 years ago. The smear campaign saw the woman's dance business closed down. Then, when the girl re-joined the jazz ballet school and won the blue ribbon for 'Dancer of the Year,' the jealous Girl Mom told people that the contest was rigged.

It's a nasty world out there, especially for mothers of daughters! On a lighter note: Girl Moms get very excited when they see a girl with sparkly hair clips and will race after the girl's mother to find out where she can purchase those clips. "It's a girl thing," explains Girl Mom to Boy Mom. "You wouldn't understand."

"It's okay for you. You can afford a cleaner," moans Jealous Mom.

JEALOUS MOM

(DGA – green, green, green – with envy)

J ealous Mom thinks everyone's got it better than her. She hates success of any kind – unless it's hers and hers alone. She's very possessive of her friends and their friendships. She hates to share anything. If she introduces one mom friend to another and those two women catch up without her, she will either give them both the silent treatment, or drop them both forever. If she has sons, she is jealous of Girl Mom. If she has girls, she is jealous of Boy Mom. Everyone else's husband is richer, better looking, or drives a better car. She even gets jealous if a woman brags about her husband's prowess in the kitchen. "Your husband makes mushroom risotto, mine can barely boil an egg," says Jealous Mom.

If her daughter is a brunette, she is jealous of mothers with blonde girls. If her son is blonde, she is jealous of moms with brunette sons. Her kids are talented musicians but that doesn't mean she is not jealous of the moms whose kids excel at chess, football or gymnastics. She takes everything very, very personally. When Scream From The Sidelines Mom posted a photo on Facebook of her son kicking a goal, Jealous Mom was upset that the photo made her own child look like a loser because he hadn't kicked a goal. When her son eventually did kick a goal, Jealous Mom decided not to post his photo on Facebook, for fear of upsetting other mothers whose kid might not have done so well. The thing is: other mothers would not have minded. Only Jealous Mom lets things like this get to her. Deeply.

Jealous Mom is very complicated. She likes to hang out with Chardonnay Mom. Then again, *everybody* likes to hang out with Chardonnay Mom.

"It's all too hard – the kids, the housework, the husband...everything! I wish I'd never done it," cries Endurance Mom.

∽

ENDURANCE MOM

(DGA – does not stop whinging about motherhood)

∽

Endurance Mom thinks motherhood is a gigantic burden. She is always moaning and groaning about how hard it is being a mother. She lives for the day the kids are old enough to go to school. She always speaks nostalgically about her precious 'pre-mom days'. "Remember when you could go shopping alone? I could travel at the drop of a hat. I had sex whenever I felt like it. I've gotten so used to kissing the kids' faces that it feels weird kissing my husband's face with its stubble. I'm not just a mom; I'm a woman!" she cries. Fertility Mom wants to slap her. "Don't you know how lucky you are to have kids in the first place?" she asks. Endurance Mom likes to seek out work that takes her away from her family; but she quickly realizes that the job hasn't changed – she has.

These women do *not* fantasize about having more children. These women make a great deal of fuss about the amount of 'Me Time' they manage to achieve. It wouldn't cross their minds that, prior to having kids, they had at least 25 or maybe 40 years of 'Me Time'. "I can't wait until Joshua is potty trained. I can't wait until he goes to school. I can't wait until he's at college. Hell, I can't wait until he's overseas travelling the world and meeting his wife so she can take over," said one Endurance Mom. They are particularly amazed by Adoption Mom because they cannot imagine somebody actually wanting children so much that they would take such drastic and unselfish measures to be a mother. She can be seen at the gym with Buns of Steel Mom, pretending that they don't have children.

"Kids? What kids? Oh yeah. I've got three! Sometimes I just forget," says Jackass Mom.

JACKASS MOM

(DGA – she sits in the car texting her friends while the kids are paddling in the ocean moments after a shark alert)

Jackass Mom has half a brain. She will leave aspirin lying around house, she smokes in front of her kids, she thinks nothing of lighting up in the car with all the windows shut; it's a free world isn't it? She will leave her baby in a stroller at the cliff's edge with the brake open. If her child is ill, she gives out paracetamol without checking the measurements so always gives either too little or too much. Her idea of supervising kids in a swimming pool is to stand in the kitchen doing the dishes or chatting on the phone and looking up every five minutes. She leaves a chair beside the pool gate. "That's so I don't have to keep opening the damn gate. The kids can just stand on the chair and open it whenever they like," said Jackass Mom.

Once she let go of the stroller at the bus stop and it rolled onto the highway and narrowly missed being hit by a bus. A teenager happened to record it on his phone and it ended up on the nightly news. Yet, instead of being shocked or embarrassed, she emailed the YouTube link to her family and friends. Steak knives are left on the kitchen bench, she wouldn't dream of doing something as simple as turning the saucepan handle away from a toddler's grasp, she puts vodka in a kids Spiderman Sippy cup (to hide her drinking problem from her husband) and thinks it's hilarious when her three year old takes a swig thinking it's water.

"Right, Balthazar, that's it! Stop throwing sand at your sister! That's your fifth naughty cross for today. Say goodbye to the beach. Home now! You've got a date with the naughty chair!" screams Punishment Mom.

∽

PUNISHMENT MOM

(DGA – her kids automatically stand
in the corner even before they are told to)

∽

From the naughty stair to the dreaded 'corner', Punishment Mom thrives on creating new ways to teach her kids a lesson! Chili on the tongue, check! Star charts, check! The naughty chart, check! It's simple; every time you do something bad you get a cross and when you have five crosses you are punished. Popular punishments include:

You are not allowed to play with friends. You are not allowed on the next family camping trip (note: Thomas will stay with grandparents). Whack on leg so hard it leaves a red hand print. Teddy taken away and so child can't sleep. Then blanky taken away! Time out, five minutes if you're five years old. Her son is made to stand in corner because his new sneakers were making annoying squeaking sounds on the tile floor. Her daughter is forced to stand in the corner because she accidently dropped her juice on the tile floor. Her toddler is told to stand in corner because he slipped in the juice on the tile floor and broke the glass.

Punishment Mom gets very excited when she creates a new punishment. For her, it is a creative process similar to that followed by film makers and authors. "I told him if he is naughty, Santa will hate him. If he uses rude words again, he won't be allowed to use the toilet for a week, and he'll have to pee in the garden," said Punishment Mom. *Supernanny* is their God of choice. They take notes during the show and take her advice to heart. One Punishment Mom said her favorite punishment is to ban her son from attending a friend's birthday party. "It is a very effective punishment," she insists. "It has longevity. He's upset on the day of the party but on Monday at school, while his friends are talking about the party that he missed out on, he gets upset all over again. It works by forcing him to think about his appalling behavior". Usually Punishment Mom is so busy focussing on the punishment given; she has forgotten exactly what the kid did that was so dreadful in the first place.

"Did she say Balthazar? That poor child! Imagine living with a name like that!" says Name Police Mom.

৵

NAME POLICE MOM

(DGA – the first thing she'll ask you is "What's your kid's name?" She also carries a baby name dictionary so she can tell people what their child's name actually means)

৵

N ame Police Mom has an opinion on every child's name, whether you named him John or Banjo, Jane or September. Name Police Mom confronted a pregnant woman, asking her if she has chosen a name.

"Luke," said Poor Me Mom.

"Boring! Surely you can do better than that?" said Name Police Mom. "And what's your toddler's name?"

"Dashiell," said Poor Me Mom.

"Urg! Don't you know that means 'peasant boy?' And anyway, you're just copying that movie star, Cate Blanchett. She has a Dashiell. Show some originality. What about your other kid?" asked Name Police Mom.

"Xavier," whispers Poor Me Mom. "Xavier! My God, how's the poor kid ever going to learn to spell that?"

Of course, her own child's name is perfect and don't even bother trying to tell her otherwise. She will tell you she was the first person to call her daughter Sienna and everybody else just copied her. She particularly hates the trend of giving your child a surname as a Christian name, such as Fletcher, Taylor and Gibson. She wishes she could arrest the parents. If only she could.

"My child's name is Moonbeam Sky Lark," says Extreme Alternative Mom.

EXTREME ALTERNATIVE MOM

(DGA – she keeps empty ice cream containers in her car, in case her baby has a 'little accident')

Extreme Alternative Mom is endlessly fascinating as she delights in shocking people with her radical behavior. She doesn't use diapers, she still breastfeeds her four year old, she home schools the kids and thinks everyone else is wrong. Maybe she's right? Maybe not. She does not immunize her children but admits, if every mother followed her lead and refused to immunize their kids it would mean diseases like polio could return, she'd be first in queue at the doctors. But, for now, she aligns closely with My Child's Body is a Temple Mom by insisting her kid gets a 'free ride' on everybody else's immunisation.

Extreme Alternative Mom went to a friend's house and held her four week old baby above the woman's kitchen sink so the bub could pee in it. "AGH! I wash the dishes in there!" said Poor me Mom. Extreme Alternative Mom buys the theory that babies do not need diapers and that even a five minutes old baby has control of its bowels. She carries an empty ice cream container with her for 'little emergencies'. She even rides the bus with her baby in one arm and the 'portable potty' in the other, to collect its pee....much to the horror of the passengers. However, if you delve deep, even the staunchest Extreme Alternative Mom can be beaten in an argument. Just ask them what they do instead of diapers when the baby is asleep and, if you keep pushing, they will reluctantly admit that YES they do use a diaper, but only between the hours of 10:00 pm and 3:00 am. No diapers? Hmm. She constantly has poo on her hands and gives Germ Phobic Mom the horrors.

"Never put your bare hand on a door handle. You never know – the last person that touched it might have a disease! Always use a cloth," says Germ Phobic Mom.

GERM PHOBIC MOM

(DGA – a bottle of disinfectant in her handbag)

Germ Phobic Mom gasps in horror if another toddler takes a sip from her child's cup ... only to be seen quickly wiping the mouthpiece with a muslin wrap and then packing it out of reach of their own darling. If your child so much as *sneezes* in the same air space as Germ Phobic Mom she will whisk her little precious to the far regions of the playground, lest he catch whatever horror bug your child has been carelessly 'sharing'. The offspring of Germ Phobic Mom risk growing up to be germophobes of Howard Hughes' proportions (Hughes wore tissue boxes on his feet and burned his clothes if he came in contact with an ill person). Germ Phobic Mom is always in the ear of Cold Blaming Mom.

This mom will not let her kids swim in a public pool due to the bacteria in the water, not to mention the hidden horrors (urine). She will not let her kids play on public play equipment. However some Germ Phobic Moms make sure they get to the playground at the crack of dawn and spray the equipment with disinfectant before letting their child have a go on the swings/slide/monkey bars. Luckily, most Germ Phobic Moms grow out of their warped ways by the time their child reaches puberty and they accept that they are in charge of their own fate; if they don't wash their hands after touching a door knob then they must suffer the consequences.

"Who the hell gave my kid a cold? Just wait until I find out who it was," warns Cold Blaming Mom.

COLD BLAMING MOM

(DGA – if her kid gets sick, she works the phone trying to track down the perpetrator)

Cold Blaming Mom is on a mission to track down the child who could have possibly given her little darling a cold. At the first sign of a cough or runny nose, Cold Blaming Mom will go through her weekly diary and narrow down the play-date/child that could have possibly passed a nasty lurgy onto her child. She then will send nasty text messages to the mother. That's usually where that friendship ends. She seems to think that mothers deliberately let their sick children loose on society in a bid to spread illness. If you try and reason with her (she could be standing in the supermarket queue and a stranger might sneeze and innocently pass on his illness) she will tell you that you're missing the point.

A Cold Blaming Mom invited a friend to her home. Her friend's child had recently recovered from the flu.

Within a week, Cold Blaming Mom's kids came down with the flu and she got herself worked up into such a rage, where she accused her friend of deliberately spreading the flu. The two women have never spoken again. These moms are also lacking in empathy for any mother or child coping with an illness of any kind; from cancer to the common cold. They will never say, 'Oh, you poor thing. Is there anything I can do to help you?" These ladies do not mince words. She is more likely to say, "You're sick? Don't you dare come near my kids!" Cold Blaming Mom is one of the most ruthless of mothers and is usually found in the company of ER Mom and Organic Mom.

"So long as everybody else keeps immunizing their kids, I won't be immunizing mine. There's no need to put all those nasty chemicals in their pure bodies if they're not even at risk!" says My Child's Body is a Temple Mom.

MY CHILD'S BODY IS A TEMPLE MOM

(DGA – her kid stays away from school
if there's an outbreak of whooping cough)

M y Child's Body is a Temple Mom will not let anything less than 100% purity pass her child's lips. She will not give her child anything sweeter than an apple and, no matter how sick the child is, will not administer any pain relief. This is because if the child has a headache or fever, giving the child an aspirin will mask the symptoms. Of course, she will not immunize her child. When confronted by a member of the medical profession, she comes up with a list of justification for her actions – from "He might get autism," to "He might be the 0.01% of kids who actually catch mumps from the injection". When pushed, she reluctantly admits she has to rely on the great majority of parents to immunize their child, because if *nobody* immunized their kids, even the dreaded diphtheria would make a comeback.

The more extreme type of My Child's Body is a Temple Mom will also religiously guard her child from putting anything 'bad' in his mouth; he is on a strict diet, with no processed foods, salt or sugar. "There's nothing but natural sugar in my son's body!" she gloats. He has never tried a muffin, a chocolate, or ice-cream. His list of 'have nots' is long and depressing. His mother won't even let him nibble a sausage because, "It is inferior meat, made from pigs' ears and noses". But when her child is allowed to visit a friend's house, he gorges himself on all the forbidden food, such as the humble muesli bar. These kids usually end up obese as teenagers when they are finally free to 'abuse their bodies' the way their friends have been abusing theirs since childhood.

"Throw the ball to Lisa, darling," says Best Friend Mom.

౼

BEST FRIEND MOM

(DGA – she doesn't let her kids call her 'Mom')

౼

B est Friend Mom wants to be seen as a Cool Mom who is less of a mother, more of a close friend. She never disciplines her child, preferring to gently remind them of their wrong doings. She is sugar sweet to her kids; you will never hear her raise her voice. This mom is literally killing her kids with kindness. She is mother to the most pampered and annoying kids on the street. She usually insists on her kids calling her by her Christian name. Anything the kids want, she will get for them. If they've just had their second ice-cream/candy bar, if they want a third, they'll get it. If her son whacks another kid, this mom will barely stop short of congratulating him for his excellent fighting skills. "My Zack is champion boxer in the making!" she says.

She has the ability to turn every single situation into a positive one. Bad grades at school? That just means you're going to be a sporting superstar. The kid is not sporty and has bad grades? No problem, he will be a famous artist! There is no room for reality in this mom's world. But if any other kid hits her kid – beware. She will berate the other child for being violent and lecture the other mom for raising an aggressive child. If her child is naughty, Best Friend Mom will gently tell her that his behavior was just 'a tiny bit inappropriate'. Yet he will not be punished. He will simply be reminded that in life, "We all have choices and the right to express ourselves". Best Friend Mom is in her element when their kids become teenagers. She loves nothing more than joining her daughter on shopping outings and not only 'Oohs and Aahs" over her fabulous taste in clothing but will not discourage her from choosing sexy attire and buying a larger size for herself to wear.

Best Friend Mom of boys has to struggle to be included in her sons' activities once they hit the teenage years. But she will try her best to muscle her way into joining them with their friends at the movies. Or, she will hang out, from a short distance, at the Mall when they go cruising for girls.

"Life begins at 40. Forty is the new 30!" says Older Mom.

OLDER MOM

(DGA – she is excited about getting tickets to a Bruce Springsteen concert)

Older Mom loves to lecture Younger Mom about the advantages of 'leaving it until later'; particularly in the areas of, 'I have travelled the world' and 'I have already had my brilliant career'. Older Moms are usually as addicted to the gym as Buns of Steel Moms because they have to work that extra bit harder to maintain their fitness levels; many are mid 40s-plus and still chasing toddlers in the park. Older Mom dislikes Younger Mom as much as Younger Mom dislikes Older Mom. It's almost impossible for them to *not* speak in a condescending voice when they say, "When I was your age I was the China correspondent for an international TV station and also hosted my own radio show which once was broadcast live from Tiananmen Square".

They also like to brag about the many years they had with their partner, travelling the world and virtually growing up together, before they had children. Of course there is the other extreme; many Older Moms are in this category of motherhood because they either waited until it was almost too late to meet a partner and have kids...or that they just got lucky at the tail end of their reproductive years. If they fall in this latter group, Older Moms will brag to Younger Moms (and anybody else who cares to listen) about the great advantages of finding love in the September of their lives; that they'd had enough crappy relationships in their 20s and 30s to know what Mr Right looks like.

There is one thing that will shut up Older Mom when she is lecturing Younger Mom....that is when Younger Mom points out that her kids grandmother is the same age as Older Mom. "My mother loves being a Nanna but she never babysits for me. You see, she's only 42 so she's still working fulltime," said Younger Mom. Ouch.

"Forty? My God, that's another 15 years away for me! By the time my kids are 18 I'll still be young enough to start a new career!" says Younger Mom.

YOUNGER MOM

(DGA – she dresses like a teenager because she is a teenager)

These women snap like killer dogs when Older Mom, assuming they are single moms, ask, "Is the father still around?" Younger Mom can't wipe the smile from her face as she watches the 40-something moms desperately trying to chase rogue toddlers; panting for breath doing a second lap around the supermarket. Younger Moms loves to make thinly veiled caustic comments to Older Moms along the lines of, "Oh, aren't you a nice Nanna to take her to playground!" The less inhibited Younger Mom will cut to the chase and ask, 'Are you the Grandmother?" "No! I'm her mother!" says Older Mom. "And what are you...the nanny? Or is this your baby sister? Are you on school holidays?"

Younger Moms love to rub in the fact that they are still young enough to go out partying at night, with their kid's grandmother babysitting. Also, they're still of an age where they are chatted-up by men and enjoy recounting their night's adventures when they're standing outside the classrooms waiting for the school bell to ring. Younger Moms take great pleasure in letting Older Moms know that they are young enough that when the kids are older, they're still employable and not having to lie about their age like the tragic Older Moms are often forced to. Younger Mom lets Older Mom know that they still have their best years ahead of them. When their kids are grown up, Younger Mom will still be at an age to take a trip around Europe while Older Mom will be on the verge of entering a retirement village. The truth hurts.

"She might be 40, but she still looks hotter than me," says Sloth Mom.

∽

SLOTH MOM

(DGA – she still wears the same sweat pants she wore to the hospital en route to giving birth)

∽

Sloth Mom might once have been a beautiful butterfly, but she is now a caterpillar. For these women, stepping into motherhood has meant redefining the word 'plain'. They only shop at convenience stores or mass-produced clothing stores. Make-up is a word they kissed goodbye the moment their babies were born. Gone are the days when these women would dab a bit of concealer over a new pimple, apply a layer of mascara or wipe some pink lip gloss over their lips. These moms have gone the way some women/men do in the days following a wedding…now they have got their man/woman they feel they can rest easy, the chase is over they don't need to try anymore. A hair brush? Forget about it. Blush? Foundation? What's that again? Men look at them and wonder, hmm what would she have looked like pre-kids? It's the female equivalent of men who 'let themselves go' once they meet the woman of their dreams, putting on weight and wearing sweats and little else.

Sloth Moms let themselves go when they achieve their dream of becoming a mom. They already have what they searched for all their life, so there's no need to make an impression. Her idea of dressing up is to wear the same dirty jeans and blue sweater she's been wearing all week but she'd add a pink scarf for that extra bit of oomph. Don't even waste your breath suggesting they replace those buttons, get a new pair of jeans once the hole in the knee is bigger than fist size ... they are not interested in anything to do with personal grooming. Strangely, most Sloth Moms make sure their kids look a million bucks, perhaps in the hope some of their style will be reflected back at them.

"I haven't even looked in a mirror for two years,"
says Multiple Mom, pushing her triplet stroller.

MULTIPLE MOM

(DGA – there's a 'Triplets
on Board' sticker on her SUV)

Multiple Mom is the mother of twins/triplets or, God forbid, quadruplets or more. These are the only mothers of whom all other mothers are in awe. The only exception is Olympic Mom who refuses to believe that giving birth to more than one child at once could be more challenging than just one at a time. Multiple Mom is usually highly organized but, unlike Bootcamp Mom, don't make a big deal about it.

A mother of triplets can usually get her three babies in and out of a car faster than the mother of a singleton child, simply because she *has* to be fast. Multiple Mom rolls her eyes when mothers of singleton children complain. If only they knew how easy it was to be pregnant with just one child, or to breastfeed just one child, or to get up in the night to just one screaming baby. There is a hierarchy in the Multiple Mom breed: a twin mother might be accustomed to bragging to singleton moms about giving birth to kids two minutes apart...but in the presence of a Higher Order Multiple Mom she will concede defeat and admit that she 'only gave birth to two at once'.

Multiple Mom is usually the most thankful to be mothers for the simple reason many of them might have undergone fertility treatment as a last resort. These women see having two or three at once as their 'reward' for going through all the crap (fertility issues) most women luckily avoid. Multiple moms also have very thick skins as they have to endure the relentless questions from singleton mothers; "Are your kids natural?" One Multiple Mom claims to have every comeback in the book but usually replies with, "No, they are *plastic*".

"Andrew, Sophia, Oscar! Home play is in 12 minutes. Come here NOW! We have five minutes to get into the car and home," shouts Bootcamp Mom.

∽

BOOTCAMP MOM

(DGA – her kids stand to attention.
If they knew how to, they would salute too)

∽

Bootcamp Mom is the ultimate stickler for a routine. A child must rise no later than 6:30am; he/she must eat breakfast 45 minutes later, then drink a glass of milk, then get in the car and spend 30 minutes in the park, then return for home playtime at 11:30am, then eat lunch at 12:15pm and so on. She has a very strict sleep routine; regardless of whether the child is tired. One Bootcamp Mom was so distraught when child number three went to hospital with pneumonia – not because she was worried about his well-being – but because it meant that her routine was thrown severely out of whack. In fact, she discharged him from hospital early, and against the advice of doctors, just so she could have dinner on the table at 6:00pm, followed by bath time at 6:30, story time at 7:00, lights out at 7:30pm.

When the kids are in bed she makes their sandwiches for the next day, simply because she would panic if the mere ten minutes it takes to get the lunches ready would disrupt her routine. She expects all her mommy friends to fit in with her schedule. If somebody dares suggest a midday catch-up in the park, Bootcamp Mom will not budge from her routine. "Sophia sleeps from 11:50 until 12:45. Not a minute more, not a minute less!" says Bootcamp Mom. This woman is so set in her routine that kids have to eat when she tells them to eat; not when they are hungry. There are simply no exceptions to her rules; not Christmas, not Easter, not Halloween. Sadly, her kids emerge from childhood so tightly bound in the routine strait jacket they cannot help but rebel. Her role model is Captain von Trapp from *The Sound of Music*, in his pre-Maria days, when he still controlled his kids with a whistle.

"Is it wine time already? I've got a bottle of Jacob's Creek in the fridge. All welcome!" says Chardonnay Mom.

∾

CHARDONNAY MOM

(DGA – bottle opener and corks in her handbag)

∾

C hardonnay Mom loves to pour her first glass at 'wine o'clock', claiming it's the only way to get through the witching hour consisting of cooking, feeding, bathing and bedtime. She will constantly invite moms over for a 'party' – any excuse to crack open the bubbly. Chardonnay Mom is a big fan of the champagne breakfast and will go to great lengths to organize mommy get-togethers after school drop-off, on the off chance somebody will bring a bottle of wine so that she can get that special buzz early in the day.

This mom never got out of the habit of the 'Thank God it's Friday' drinks that she used to enjoy to excess during her pre-mom days. Instead of departing the workplace with a handful of colleagues and traipsing to the nearest bar, these days Chardonnay Mom will organize 'after school drinkies' at various mom's homes, where she leads the ladies in the fine art of getting sozzled while the kids run amok in the backyard. These drinks parties usually wind up by 6:00pm so the moms can get kids home to be fed, bathed and put into bed. There is a chorus of, "Are you okay to drive?" and then a stampede of women stagger to the kitchen where they guzzle large glasses of water, as if that is enough to lower their blood alcohol ratio. The only time it isn't good to be friends with Chardonnay Mom is when she promises beforehand to be the designated driver. It's never going to happen.

Chardonnay Mom is also the first person at school fundraising nights who will get up onstage with the band, flash her underwear and sing the first verse of the national anthem over and over, until she collapses in a heap of emotion; usually crying about the beauty of the night and bemoaning the fact the staff has left and the bar is closed.

"My kids make their own dinner. I trained them to be independent the moment they could walk," says Lazy Mom.

∽

LAZY MOM

(DGA – she pays a college student to pick the kids up from school because the school bell clashes with her favorite soap opera)

∽

Lazy Mom will only take her kids to the park once a fortnight and will never let them do anything after school. They have the same sandwich (tomato and cheese) for lunch day after day. At home, the TV is permanently on as 'the electronic babysitter'. She will only let her kids attend a friend's birthday party if she can convince another mother to drop them there and pick them up again. She makes their school lunches twelve hours before they are eaten. So what if the tomato has made the (stale) bread soggy? That's life!

Her kids cannot tie their shoelaces because she is too lazy to teach them. Her kids are behind in their school work because Lazy Mom is 'too busy' (watching her favorite soap opera) to help them write a speech about the nation's system of governance. Her daughter had head lice for several weeks before Lazy Mom bothered to buy lice treatment and spend two hours combing and cutting – and only because the lice had jumped to *her* hair and the itching was driving her crazy. Her kids accepted a long time ago that their mother will never play with them; they have to play around her. The only reason she got pregnant in the first place is because she was too lazy to get up, walk to the bathroom and get her contraceptive pill out of the bathroom cabinet.

"Did someone say 'wine time'? Count me in. Can you take Coco and Max with you and I'll run a few errands and meet you at your place in a couple of hours. I just need some time away from the kids...you know...'Me Time', thanks!" says Runaway Mom.

RUNAWAY MOM

(DGA – returns to work when her baby is under three months old and admits she does not need the money)

Runaway Mom couldn't wait to run away from her offspring and get back to work. Some women wait until their child is as 'old' as three months before she is shunted into day-care or into the care of a grandmother or nanny. These women reassure themselves; "The kid got two months worth of breast milk. According to the latest research, that's all a baby needs". Runaway Mom is obsessed about getting precious child free time. When she is with the kids she is usually on the phone lining up babysitters/nannies/helpers to take the kids off her hands.

If Runaway Moms don't already have a job they will spend a lot of time hunting for one. If they have no urgent financial need to work then they will find something else such as oil painting classes, languages or exercise to get them away from their kids. They don't really like hanging out with other moms because that might give them a twinge of guilt. But maybe not. They get on pretty well with Endurance Mom and Office Mom. Runaway Mom thinks she is very clever taking advantage of her mom friends by dropping her kids off at their house so she can go off and shop alone. She dreams about the day her kids get their drivers' licence and are off her hands once and for all!

"I'll just come for a little while. I've hardly spent any quality time with my kids this week," says Guilt-Ridden Mom.

∽

GUILT-RIDDEN MOM

(DGA – she is always apologizing to her kids)

∽

Guilt-Ridden Mom has sleepless nights if she puts her child in front of television for more than ten minutes, just so she can get on the computer and reply to a few emails. If Guilt-Ridden Mom has a shower, she feels guilty for neglecting her kids. If she reads five books to her kids at night she feels guilty that she didn't read a sixth book. If one of her kids gets a cold, she feels guilty because it must be her fault. "Oh no, I haven't been giving them enough Vitamin C!" she cries.

If the kids aren't doing well at school, she blames herself for not bringing in a private tutor. If her kids whack each other during an argument, she feels guilty for exposing them to violent cartoons. She feels guilty that she had to have a C-section. She feels guilty she didn't breastfeed for as long as Breastfeeding Supremacist Mom.

She feels guilty that when she was carrying her baby in a sling, he got whacked by a rogue football and had a black eye at the age of four weeks. Guilt-Ridden Mom even feels tremendous guilt about her husband; that she is so preoccupied with the kids that she forgets to ask him if he'd like his feet massaged at the end of a long day in the office. Yet, if she found time to massage his feet, she'd feel guilty it was not as good as the last massage and might push him into the hands of the Thai ladies in the city who run the reflexology joint. The guilt-list is endless and this woman is constantly emotionally exhausted. Her friend, Botox Mom, is always telling her, "You've gotta do something about those frown lines!"

"My forehead is as smooth as a baby's ... but I haven't had any work. I promise!" says Botox Mom.

❧

BOTOX MOM

(DGA – she has five kids and zero wrinkles)

❧

Botox Mom is more glamorous now than she was pre-kids. It's all about high fashion and expensive face creams/surgery/Botox. They are the ultimate Glam moms. Other moms look at them with great suspicion, "Wow I can't believe you're 37 and have four kids and NO wrinkles. Amazing! Are you sure you haven't had any work done?" they ask. "No, not me! I'm just lucky I inherited great skin from my mother. She's 65 and looks 50," said Botox Mom.

One Botox Mom admits that a disadvantage to her wrinkle-free face is when she's angry with the kids; she has to really YELL because her face shows no emotion. "They can't tell, just by looking at me, whether my 'cross face' is any different to my 'happy face'" she said. Another Botox Mom was forced to take her three year old to a top-up appointment and afterwards, at the supermarket, she bumped into Sloth Mom who enquired, as they all do, whether Botox Mom has ever used Botox. Suddenly the three year old yelled, "Mommy got a needle in her face!" "Don't worry, your secret is safe with me," said Sloth Mom, before spreading it around the neighborhood. "Ahhh," said Housewife Mom. "*That's* why she looks so good."

"This job is much harder than going to the office. I'd go to the office for a break!" says Housewife Mom.

HOUSEWIFE MOM

(DGA – sweat pants, minimal makeup, spends a lot of time at the park and the supermarket)

Housewife Mom is always moaning about her tough life. It's all because she ditched her beloved career to stay at home with the kids. She likes reminding Office Mom that she is only in the kids' faces at the weekend. "During the week, you give your kids to someone else to look after!" says Housewife Mom. Many of these women look enviously at Office Mom as she hurriedly drops the kids at school and moves into another world; the world she herself once inhabited. Some Housewife Moms look at Office Moms with pity; feeling sorry that they miss out on their children's younger years. Housewife Mom likes to tell herself that being a mom is much tougher than working. If work fails that's ok, but if you fail your kids ... that's a burden that will pass on for generations.

They also like to gripe that Office Moms only work to provide for fancy holidays, investment properties and designer clothes. If you listen to the whispers from the under-dressed moms at school drop off, you will hear a running commentary about the various Office Mom outfits; "Her skirt is too short," "Check out the red suit. She's got legs up to her armpits. I bet she's screwing her boss". "That dress is so 2009," says Fashionista Mom. They like telling Office Mom that she has it easy. "You get rid of your kids for the day, you get to put on nice clothes and work in an office – and you get to interact with men who are not your husband!"

"Did you see Sloth Mom today? I swear she wears the same sweat pants every day. I wouldn't be seen dead in those!" says Fashionista Mom.

❧

FASHIONISTA MOM

(DGA – if it was on the runway this week, it'll be on this mom next week)

❧

As young women, these mothers craved attention for their appearance and, in middle age, they crave it even more. Fashionista Mom wouldn't be caught dead dressing her child in non-designer brands. She will not buy clothes unless there is an almost identical mini-me outfit. Her idea of devastation is if she wears a perfect outfit, matching with her daughter and nobody stares admiringly at them.

Fashionista Mom will wear one outfit for school drop off... but by pick up time, she has changed. Not only do these women dislike being seen in the same outfit twice, but they dislike being seen in the same outfit twice in one day. If she doesn't get a positive response from anybody then she will *never* wear that outfit again. The local thrift store has a designer rack of clothes supplied almost exclusively by Fashionista Mom. In fact she was horrified to see Thrift Store Mom wearing one of her cast off dresses to which she had added a band of inappropriate purple lace; totally unaware she had desecrated the frock of a hot Italian designer.

Fashionista Mom is usually a Girl Mom and, when she buys something for herself, she will not stop until she finds an identical outfit for her daughter. She laps up the comments, 'Wow, you've got a little clone,' the people say. She fails to register the sarcasm. One Fashionista Mom hates that her children look like her husband and not like her. She even dyed her child's hair blonde so they would look more alike. She was tired of people telling her the child looks like her brunette father. Ditto with the son.

"Fashionista Mom has more money than sense. That red mini dress she was wearing today was almost identical to one I found at the thrift store last week. Sure, it needed fixing but that's not the point!" says Thrift Store Mom.

THRIFT STORE MOM

(DGA – decked out in clothing that doesn't quite fit)

Thrift Store Mom prides in saying, "This outfit only cost me two bucks!" She's the worst dressed mom in town and her kids are the same; their entire wardrobe is a throwback to the 70s and 80s or whatever era is going on the '$5 and under' rack. She likes to mock women who spend hundreds of dollars on clothing, "Oh, look at her! Everything has to be *new!* There's a great op store in every suburb, you can even get a designer (i.e. Target) handbag for cheap!" One totally eccentric Thrift Store Mom once found a Halston skirt going for the top rate of $12 and she wore it to death. No matter that the skirt had holes in it, no matter it stunk of mould and she never washed it. It was a bargain. And the shoes! She wears the same pair every day, month after month. "I don't buy a new pair until the old pair is smiling," she says.

She is a huge fan of eBay and even buys second hand makeup online. Once, she bragged about getting an entire bag of barely-used Revlon foundation, blush and eye shadow for just $5. On the weekends, you'll find Thrift Store Mom scouring the local yard sales where, recently, she was thrilled to have purchased a Holly Hobbie quilt for her youngest daughter. It's anybody's guess what she does with the vast amounts of cash she saves by being so frugal. A trip to Paris? A new laptop? Or maybe her annual facial.

"I got these from K-Mart last week. What do you think?" asks Shoplifting Mom.

SHOPLIFTING MOM

(DGA – her husband is broke, she is unemployed yet she is always 'buying' stuff)

Shoplifting Mom takes great delight in stealing things and hiding the loot in the stroller. Look what she's got! Makeup, jewelry, perfume, books, Nike runners and even an eyelash curler. When one Shoplifting Mom was caught by the store detectives, she played the 'post natal depression' card, saying she was so depressed she needed to steal baby items to take her mind off the baby blues. The detective failed to notice she had not stolen any baby items at all. Another Shoplifting Mom bragged that she never had to buy cosmetics. She would go to Target and load up her baby stroller with mascara, foundation, powder, blush and five different brands of lip-gloss. "If you hide the loot under a stinking wet diaper, no store detective is going to look," she said.

Shoplifting Mom usually justifies her stolen goods by purchasing at least one expensive item. "I spent $280 on a new camera, so it's not like the store wasn't taking some money off *me*!" When/if Shoplifting Mom is caught, she blames the child. "He took it off the shelf when I wasn't looking." Her nine month old has great taste in stilettos. Wow! He even knew her size.

"Cool. Is there a sale on?I need a new dress. I really do. Don't you?" asks Shopaholic Mom.

∽

SHOPAHOLIC MOM

(DGA – she practically lives at the Mall and always has a department store bag under her arm)

∽

Shopaholic Mom is earning no money but is helping keep Wal-Mart afloat by making twice daily trips just to get out of the house. She hangs out with Outdoor Mom and together they paint the town red. These women shopped til they dropped when they were career girls and like to live their lives like nothing has changed. Husband earns less than you did when you were working full-time? Not an issue! Shopaholic Mom revolves her life, and her kids' lives, around the Mall.

When she drops the older kids at school she forces her baby and toddler to ride from store to store in search of a bargain. Or maybe not. Some of these moms don't like sale time and prefer to buy something for the full price just for the hell of it. Others don't care if a dress cost $10 or $300...just so long as it's a store bought item that comes in a bag that you can take home and unwrap and love until the next day and the next shopping jaunt. Shopaholic Mom trains her kids to tell their father what they didn't do that day. Instead of telling their Dad that they spent the better half of the day being wheeled around the stores, Shopaholic Mom is the queen of bribery and will tell her toddler that if she tells Daddy, "We went to the park today", then she actually *will* be allowed to go to the park. Sometime very, very soon.

It's not unusual for Shopaholic Mom to spend the bulk of her housekeeping money on a Monday, then she will be at the stores again on the Wednesday to get her 'second round' of groceries, on Thursday she will take the kids to the Mall because there's a clothing sale on and kids just 'love' watching mom try on a selection of new jeans.

There is a loud crash, followed by piercing screams. All eyes narrow and turn to Devil Spawn Mom. "Lucas, who made that noise? Of course it wasn't you honey. Just tell Mommy who did the naughty thing and I'll tell them off," says Devil Spawn Mom.

DEVIL SPAWN MOM

(DGA – bite marks on her ankles)

Devil Spawn Mom has mothered kids who are absolute terrors – the evil children you never want to invite to your house. Yet the mother, for reasons quite unknown, always believes her child is an angel. Devil Spawn Mom spied her child about to throw a baseball at a crowd of people. She didn't try to stop him. So he threw the ball, narrowly missing an elderly man. It was only when he aimed the ball for her head that she said, gently, "Hamish, what are you doing sweetheart? You wouldn't hurt Mommy, would you?" before the ball smacked her in the face, causing her to yelp in pain. But did she tell him off? No, of course not... it was an 'accident.'

These kids kick, scream, pour orange juice over the carpet and wipe yogurt on the sofa. They rub peanut butter or honey or whatever dark or sticky condiment they can get their grubby hands on over walls, picture frames and televisions. They will even find their way into the master bedroom and rub it on your pillow (by the way, none of this is an accident!). Yet the Devil Spawn Mom believes her child is a sweetheart and cannot understand why he is never invited on play dates.

"If my kids are invited to play at a friend's house, I like to come along too. The family that plays together, stays together!" says Helicopter Mom.

∾

HELICOPTER MOM

(DGA – she swims with her
kids at their swimming lesson)

∾

Helicopter Mom hovers around her kids and never leaves them alone. They are over-involved in every aspect of their kids' lives; from their sleeping habits and food to their reading tastes and friend choices. One Helicopter Mom even keeps a dream journal – a sweet idea when the kids are young – but, ten years on, she still quizzes her teenagers every morning about what they dreamt about the night before. If they say, "I don't remember," she will analyze this memory loss as being a sign of deeper issues. If her kids are playing soccer, she volunteers to be the coach. If one of her kids befriends an autistic child, she will research autism so she can better understand her kids' friend.

Some Helicopter Moms home-school their kids because they cannot handle somebody else taking charge of their child's educational development. It is not unusual for Helicopter Mom to join her kids at play dates so she can eavesdrop on the kids' conversations, as well as keeping an eye out on what the other mother is giving her kid for afternoon tea. One Helicopter Mom has become her son's classroom's unofficial 'teacher' – running errands for the real teacher and generally getting in the way. When the teacher asked her to leave, she was so distraught she enrolled at teachers' college so she could qualify with a teaching certificate and attempt to infiltrate the classroom once again.

Another Helicopter Mom had a sick child so she spent two weeks sleeping on the floor beside his bed until he had recovered from the flu. The only problem was the child became accustomed to Mom sleeping on his floor and, after he recovered, he developed an anxiety about sleeping alone. So Helicopter Mom moved a single fold-up bed into his room. It's not great for her marriage but at least she can be close to her son, should he need her in the night. Oh, her son is now thirteen and she's still sleeping in his room. When Helicopter Moms become Empty Nesters, they are hit very hard. That's when they adopt a child or several cats and dogs, so they can start the process all over again.

"Relax. They'll sort it out," says Chill out Mom.

∾

CHILL OUT MOM

(DGA – her kids are still at the Mall
after dark. Oh, and they're aged under ten)

∾

C hill Out Mom is so laid back her kids would have to be on their death bed before she dragged them to a doctor. The three year-old falls two meters off the top of the playground equipment? No problem. If she's crying, she's not dead. Six year-old fell off his skateboard. "A bloody knee? Nah, He doesn't need a bandaid. The blood hasn't even reached his ankle yet." The baby is crying as she hasn't been fed in five hours. "She'll be right. It's not even lunchtime yet. They only need three meals a day, right?" The kids want to play on the street in a thunderstorm? Sure! If they want to cross the freeway and walk four blocks to the nearest park which is next to the methadone clinic while she stays at home and catches up on *The Bold and the Beautiful*, that's fine too.

Chill Out Mom doesn't often cook dinner. She teaches the kids to do everything themselves from opening the fridge (the 18 month old) to cooking an omelette (the six year-old). She has zero tolerance for women who declare that motherhood is 'difficult'. Her reasoning? Well, we don't live in the dark ages. We have diapers, we have tinned food, we have DVDs and even if the kids are fighting, they are just kids. Chill out! Her three year old fell down two flights of stairs and spent a week with a broken arm before she took him to the doctor. But her pets? If her cat is limping she is off to the vet straight away.

"If I were you, I'd take him to hospital. What if it's concussion?!" asks ER Mom.

ER MOM

(DGA – she's on first-name
basis with all the local paramedics)

ER Mom will take her kids to hospital at the slightest cough or splutter. Be warned: if your child has an illness, a rash – or even bad breath – do not let him anywhere near ER Mom or she will physically restrain him from going within a 20 meter radius from her own little darling. One ER Mom noticed her child had a red spot near his eye. Right away, she dialled 911 before accusing a nearby child of poking him with a stick and nearly blinding him. The boy was rushed to hospital where it was discovered the red spot was paint.

ER Mom carries a list of emergency numbers and has Googled every illness; memorizing the symptoms, so she can diagnose her child herself. If her child falls from swing, she is convinced he is concussed – she calls an ambulance. If her child coughs after eating a grape, she thinks he is choking – she calls an ambulance. If her child had been playing with a coin and the coin disappears, she's convinced her child has swallowed it – she calls an ambulance. Her child is wrapped in cotton balls. He will never go to school camp in case he gets bitten by a snake or spider. They would never live in a house that is more than 15 minutes away from the local hospital. ER Mom is such a regular at the hospital she is on first name basis with many of the staff and was recently invited to the hospital charity ball where she dressed up in a nurse's uniform. Imagine her delight when a *real* doctor hit on her.

"Yeah I saw your Joshua spent two nights in intensive care. I read it on Facebook," says Social Network Mom.

❧

SOCIAL NETWORK MOM

(DGA – she shakes uncontrollably if
not clutching her Smartphone at all times)

❧

Social Network Mom is on Twitter, Facebook, Instagram, Pinterest, Buzz, Bebo, Tumblr ...and chances are, if you are friends with her, you have been on there too – like it or not. This woman has hundreds of virtual mommy friends but she quickly realized the *real* friends she added on Facebook weren't friends with her much longer. Why? Because Social Network Mom loves to post status updates about the goings on in the school playground before and after the school bell tolls. "Finally saw the wife of the Hot Dad at my kid's school. She has a face like a dropped pie. How the hell did she get HIM?"

Social Network Mom is incredibly charming in person, yet she also uses Twitter to let her followers (many of whom are fellow school moms) know she is pissed at them. "Angry that my son is NOT invited to his best friend's party all because of a water gun incident that was NOT my son's fault." Yet, hours earlier, Social Network mom had reassured the mom in question that the birthday party issue is 'no big deal'. Social Network Mom loves taking her kids to the park. It's a great way to sit and update her status reports while the kids play. There are always plenty of other moms in the park; surely they won't mind keeping an eye out on her kids while she's glued to her Smartphone?

One Social Network Mom is so lacking in self esteem since joining the ranks of the Mommy Mafia, that she uses social networking sites to create a false identity for herself. Little do the other moms realize that Social Network Mom is not the highly educated author of self-help books who claims to be on first-name terms with several high-profile politicians who seek out her services when they hit career rough patches. No way! This Social Network Mom never finished high school and worked in a fast food store right up to the last days of her pregnancy. Social Network mom was so mortified when approached by a mom asking, "So, my face looks like a dropped pie?" that she fled the area and was last seen pushing a supermarket cart with one hand, updating her Twitter on the other, colliding with an elderly lady in a wheelchair in the candy aisle, in a suburb far, far away.

"I guess you don't want to be Facebook friends with me. Do you?" asks Poor Me Mom.

∾

POOR ME MOM

(DGA – she feels desperately sorry
for herself and nobody quite knows why)

∾

Poor Me Mom thinks motherhood is a huge burden and believes she drew the short straw on everything from sleeping and feeding issues to chronic skin allergies and mental health issues. She constantly whines and moans about how hard it is being a mother and how badly the other mothers treat her. Poor Me Mom lives for the day the kids are old enough to go to school. One Poor Me Mom calls her baby daughter 'Baby Satan'. Why? Because she wakes three times a night for a feed. Well ... babies get hungry! And God forbid if that baby dirties her diaper shortly after Poor Me Mom has put on a fresh one. Oh no, Poor Me! Her friends are constantly reminding her that all other moms are in the same boat and just get on with it ... it's part of life when you're a mom.

Poor Me Mom is negative about everything – especially herself. If somebody congratulates her on her new business, she says, "It's only because I got lots of money for my divorce settlement. Did I tell you my husband left me for a Swedish super-model? Poor Me!" When a friend praised Poor Me mom's daughter's artwork, she said, "I stayed up until midnight pasting her drawings into a fancy folder and then two hours later my six month old woke up with a night fright and then my two year old wet his bed. Poor Me!"

Because her nine-year old won a school drawing contest, Poor Me Mom says, "Well I had to stay up way past my bedtime pasting his drawings into a nice folder and I'd only been in bed for two hours when my six month old woke me up because she'd kicked her covers off and was cold, and then my two-year old wet his bed. Poor Me!" Everything in this woman's life is a soap opera. Other Moms avoid asking her, "How are you?" They know they will get a lecture about all the 'dreadful' things that happened to her that day. First, one of the kids left the car door open over night so the car battery was flat and she had to wait 30 minutes for road service to arrive and jump start her car, then the baby vomited in the car, then the nine year old freaked out because a grasshopper jumped onto his lap. When the boy squealed, Poor Me Mom crashed the car into a bush and killed a duck, so all the kids bawled and they were 15 minutes late for school when the two year old peed her pants again.

Moms also know never to ask Poor Me Mom about breastfeeding, potty training or food. Apparently one of her kids is a fussy eater and Poor Me Mom has sleepless nights about the availability of gluten-free bread and mangoes – which is the only fruit her nine year old is not allergic to. Nobody wants to be friends with Poor Me Mom who will even whinge to Multiple Mom (who has triplets) about how tough her life is because she had three kids under five. "Deal with it honey. I had three kids under five minutes," said Multiple Mom. Nobody, but nobody... has it harder than Poor Me Mom.

"Oh my God! I'm still three blocks from the school and the afternoon bell has just gone ... the other kids will be out by now," wails Abduction Mom. "Strange men might be lurking by the school gate!"

 srdlo

ABDUCTION MOM

(DGA – her toddler is only allowed on the mean suburban streets if he is attached to a lead which is attached to his mother's wrist)

srdlo

Abduction Mom is paranoid to the point of lunacy that her little darling will be kidnapped. She forces her toddler to wear a harness; not to safeguard against him running into the traffic, but in case a stranger might snatch him from under her gaze. She also checks her children several times a night to make sure they have not been stolen. Her paranoia is fed via her obsession with newspapers, which she checks for any stories about kidnapping. One Abduction Mom had twin toddlers on a double harness when they managed to break free. Twin 1 ran west, Twin 2 ran south. The anguished screams of this mother could be heard a block away. When the twins were safely returned to her, she admitted she wasn't fearful of them running onto the road; she was worried they would run into the arms of a kidnapper.

Abduction Mom likes to cover her refrigerator door with photos of missing children, as a reminder that her fears are another mother's reality. But there is hope; some Abduction Moms lighten up to the extent that they purchase fun harnesses. We've all spotted those kids wearing a backpack shaped like a teddy bear, with a strap attached to it that extends to the mother's wrist. A harness cleverly disguised as a toy means that other kids will not ask, 'Why is that kid on a dog lead?'

"Wait! Ladies! Before you go...is anybody interested in a lingerie party next week?" asks Party Plan Mom.

༄

PARTY PLAN MOM

(DGA – her handbag is overflowing with Avon catalogues)

༄

Party Plan Moms are on a mission – they need to recruit other moms to join their team Tupperware/jewelry/lingerie/sex toys/Avon and they won't take NO for an answer! They will shove a catalogue under your nose and show you the latest 'special deals.' Did you know you can buy a 10 lb bucket of washing detergent for $7? What they don't tell you is that you can buy it for cheaper at the local supermarket. Party Plan mom plays hard to convince other mothers to join 'The Team. If you refuse, they will keep inviting you over and over again. But if they fail to recruit you, they will snub you and never forgive you for not succumbing to their passion.

Party Plan mom is constantly dropping invitations to educational toy evenings or even lunches, as a way to lure unsuspecting mothers into joining their 'family'. It all sounds tempting until you realize that even if you sell $2,000 worth of the products, the most you will make is $150 which barely covers the fuel and babysitting costs for the day. These women make friends fast, but they lose them even faster.

The Mommy Mafia is invisible to all– until you become a Mother too. Until then, you had no idea such a clan existed. It's like when you are hungry; the only stores you notice are the ones selling food. Beware of the Mommy Mafia....you never see them coming.

"Okay, let's go! Is everybody right to drive?" asks Chardonnay Mom, as a fleet of cars pull out into the unsuspecting traffic. The Mommy Mafia move on.

Olympic, Germ Phobic, Chardonnay, Run-Away, Lazy, Wikipedia or Bootcamp; Which Mother Are You?

If we have left you (or your friends) out of the Mommy Mafia, please let us know! Email <u>libbyjane3@ gmail.com</u>

ABOUT THE AUTHOR

The author Libby-Jane Charleston is author of popular blog The Mommy Mafia. She's the proud mother of three boys. She's also the mother of twins, the daughter of a twin, the niece of a twin and the aunt of twins. In other words, she is completed obsessed with twins and is a self-confessed Olympic Mom (warning: don't try and tell me having kids a whole year apart is *anything* like giving birth to or breastfeeding two at once!).

A journalist, she began her career as one of the youngest-ever columnists on the *West Australian* newspaper. She's the author of novel *Light Sweet Crude* and picture book *I Will Love You Until* . She's an award winning short story writer who has been a TV anchor, a Beijing correspondent, a magazine and newspaper journalist whose short stories have been published in several anthologies. She completed her Master of Arts thesis just weeks before giving birth to her twins. She's also been a catwalk model, a radio show host and a TV reporter whose specialty in Hong Kong was reporting live from the scene of typhoons – but none of this prepared her for the onslaught of twins.

9 781614 485483